Effective Prayer

Russell H. Conwell

Contents

FOREWORD

THAT prayers are answered nearly all the human race believe. But the subject has been beclouded and often made ridiculous by inconsistent superstitions.

This book is a modest attempt to clear up some of the errors. Its record is as accurate as impartial observation can make it. God is not bribed. Laziness cannot bargain with him. But the prayers of the righteous and of repentant sinners availeth much.

Desired ends are gained by prayer which cannot be gained by any other method. The daily experiences of devout persons establish that fact conclusively. The reasons
and the methods which produce the results seem hidden, and they often bewilder the investigator. God's thoughts are far above our thoughts. But we can trust our daily experience far enough to retain our confidence in the potency of prayer. It is, therefore, a profitable and comforting study.

RUSSELL H. CONWELL

Chapter I - Effect of Environment

THE fascinating history of events connected with the Baptist Temple, Philadelphia, through thirty-nine years, must be recorded carefully to obtain the credence of those readers who live out of the locality. It may or may not be that the unusual demonstrations of power, seemingly divine, were not incited or influenced by the special environment. Yet the critical reader may reasonably inquire where these things occurred in order to determine the power of association on the form and effect of prayer.

The Baptist Temple is a somewhat imposing building on the corner of North Broad and Berks streets in Philadelphia. It is located almost at the geographical center of Philadelphia, and eighteen squares north of the City Hall. The Temple is architecturally very plain, and the beautiful stained-glass windows are about the only ornaments in the great hall save, of course, the pipes of the great organ. The church is one hundred and seven feet front, and is one hundred and fifty feet in length. There is a deep gallery occupying three sides, with a chorus gallery, back of the pulpit, seating one hundred and fifty singers. There are three thousand and thirty-four opera chairs arranged in a semicircle, and every person in the congregation can see clearly the platform and chorus, and each normal worshiper can be heard from the pulpit.

The building itself is a testimonial to the effectiveness of sincere prayer. The Temple and the halls in the lower story, as it now stands, are far beyond the dreams of that little company of earnest worshipers who, in 1880, hesitatingly and embarrassed, began to build the small church at the corner of Berks and Mervine streets. They had no wealthy or influential friends. They had but little money or property; they could pray, and that they did do unceasingly. Any man who tries to describe or explain fully how it came about that the Temple was built becomes bewildered in the complications, unless he covers the whole question by saying, "The Lord did it." In six years after the small church was completed the Temple was begun on Broad Street.

For seven or eight years after its construction the Temple was a Mecca to which pilgrims seemed to come from all parts of the earth to kneel there in prayer. One Good Friday night, which was observed quite generally as a season of fasting and prayer, the writer entered by the side door the Temple at two o'clock in the morning, and in the dim light of two small gas jets, always left burning, he saw scores of people scattered through the church. Why that church had such a fascination for or preference with earnest seekers for the prayer answering God none may explain.

All were kneeling separately in silent prayer. As they passed in and out there were in the line, going and coming, Chinamen, Europeans, Orientals, and Americans from distant states. Different denominations, Protestant, Catholic, Jew, colored and white, were often represented among the individual worshipers. They also came any night in the week at any hour and prayed silently for a while and then went silently out. The church was not locked, night or day, for fifteen years. People sought the place when they sought to find a locality which was especially near to the Lord. It may be that any place is as near to God as any other; and many think it only a sentiment, superstitious and foolish, to esteem one place above another in matters of effective prayer. But there does stand out the fact that, for some good reason, devout people do feel more deeply the soul's communion with God in certain favorable places.

Why the Baptist Temple had such worship as a sentimental matter brings forward the facts that the graves of the loved, the home of childhood, the trysting places, the old fireplace, or the churches where sainted parents worshiped are influential because of the suggestions which come with sacred memories. That fact is a strong agency in the awakening of tender and sacred emotions. But the Baptist Temple was new and could lay claim to none of those associations. Men and women with no religious habits, and some seemingly without devout inclinations, testified decidedly that whenever they visited the building they felt that they had entered into an atmosphere of special spiritual and sacred power.

One soldier of the English army wrote an interesting letter in 1897, saying: "I do not recall any such impression before. I went into the church alone out of curiosity to look at its architectural design. But the moment I entered the side aisle I felt an indescribable pressure which made me desire to pray. I hurried out to the street to escape the solemn impression. But twice since then I have been in the auditorium and each time some power seemed pressing me down to my knees."

Whether that influence was the act of God or not cannot be proven by any known formula of human reasoning, and hence it remains, as most of such questions do, a matter of faith. Some believe it was a divine presence which made itself felt there, and other good men do not believe the conditions were in any way unusual or unnatural.

So many persons with uncontrolled imaginations, and others with their mental faculties weakened or distorted, often reported the most improbable visions and absurd revelations. Such characters, half insane or wholly deranged, have ever been present in every genuinely spiritual movement. So it was, and is, at the Baptist Temple. Those inconsistent, deranged advocates of religion did often drive away permanently into the ranks of unbelievers the most sincere investigators. But a calm review of the testimonies concerning the occurrences which followed so clearly the petitions they offered in the Temple seems overwhelmingly to establish the claim, now held by so many thousand people, that the results of the prayers were but a cause and natural effect, as the prayers and results were infallibly related.

It is not claimed here, however, that the place had more influence with man than other places have had. The plain facts are recorded here with great caution and with a determination to keep conservatively within the truth and draw no unreasonable conclusions. It. is a true statement, known to all the community, that many thousands of people have sought to pray in the Temple, believing that the boon their hearts desired would be more sure to be sent if they asked for it within the Temple walls. Many persons have attended the church services on the Sabbath who have been so deep in prayer that they were unconscious of the music or the preaching. We must reassert that this fact is not recorded here to sustain any idea that the Temple is a sacred place above many other churches, cathedrals, and holy places, but to sustain the opinion that there are places more sacred than others to certain people, and that burdened hearts and minds would act wisely if they sought some such place when the answer to their prayer seems especially vital.

Chapter II - How a Church was Built by Prayer

IN 1886 the small church at Mervine and Berks streets in the northern section of Philadelphia was crowded at every service. Children were turned away from every session of the Bible school, and tickets were issued a week in advance for the preaching services. The idea of moving to some larger place was discussed, as it was impossible to enlarge the building where it stood, because of the streets on three sides. Under those circumstances the people began to pray.

A voluntary committee canvassed the small band of church members, asking each to pray for an opening to a larger work. It is often thought to be an easy thing to promise to pray for a person or for a cause. The promise to pray is too often made carelessly, and disinterested auditors often feel relieved of all responsibility when, instead of a collection, they are let off with a request to pray for the advocated cause. But a sincere promise to pray for a cause carries with it the sincere purpose to work and to give self-sacrificingly. To say, "We do not ask for your money, but only that you pray for us," is a half-hypocritical request, because a real prayer can ascend only from a soul intent on doing. To agree to pray is a hearty promise also to do all in one's power to work with the Lord. Only the hearty worker can really pray. "The people had a mind to work," said Nehemiah, and God, seeing their zeal, responded to their appeal. The Lord answered in a way absolutely unforeseen. The salvation of the world cost a great sacrifice, and everywhere we see the results of a mysterious law that some must die that others may live, and that real happiness is ever gained at the cost of suffering.

A little child in Philadelphia opened the gates of the Temple by going down through death. She had been unable to get into the overcrowded Bible school one Sunday, and she began to save her pennies to help secure some larger place. Little Hattie May Wyatt, living in a home near the church, was chosen of God to convey his answer to the pleadings of that church. How little could the afflicted parents realize what **a** great work their sweet, prattling Hattie was to do in her short life. When the sweet, pale face lay in the coffin amid the flowers and tears, her pocketbook, containing fifty-seven cents which she had saved, was handed to the minister. She was the messenger of God on earth before she became one in heaven!

That fifty-seven cents was a sacred treasure, and at the next church meeting prayers went up to God, asking direction how to invest the first gift toward the larger accommodations.

One patriarch led in prayer and earnestly and asked the Lord to "take these few pennies and build for us a temple." There were some in the assembly who said, "What can this little supply do among so many?" But the most part seemed inspired with a faith that was immovable. The Lord then put a thought into the mind of John Baer, who owned a lot of land on the corner of Broad and Berks streets, to suggest to a member of the church that, as the people needed larger quarters, they ought to buy his lot and erect there a larger church. Mr. Baer did not know then that the church had only fifty-seven cents and that the church building they then occupied was still heavily mortgaged. Another church member heard of Mr. Baer's remark and, with the assurance of a faith unshakable, told Mr. Baer that if he would take fifty-seven cents as the first payment he felt sure the church would purchase it. Mr. Baer (a devout man) said that he would cheerfully accept the terms and that he would also not only give back the fifty-seven cents, but would contribute one thousand dollars toward the first payment on the lot.

The church then purchased the lot and held another prayer meeting to determine the second time what to do with the Wyatt fifty-seven cents. It was unanimously decided to organize a "Wyatt Mite Society" to invest the money. There were to be fifty-seven children in the society, and each was to invest one of the pennies so as to secure the largest possible amount for the new church. It seems almost miraculous that wherever a child tried to sell the penny not one would buy it after hearing the story, but nearly all did give a liberal donation. One lady gave fifteen hundred dollars. Finally, the pennies all came back, were put in a coin frame, and kept as a sacred souvenir. Then joyful enthusiasm seized upon the people and hurried them along in many different enterprises for raising money.

One Sabbath the pastor was over-persuaded to exchange with Doctor Pierce of Mount Holly, and the joyful people presented the pastor, on his return, with a subscription list of ten thousand dollars. But to that account the practical and critical businessman can answer that in any enterprise, enthusiasm, hard work, and economy secure success almost invariably. So that even the matter of raising one hundred and nine thousand dollars by a people, all poor, industrious persons, may not be absolutely convincing to the skeptic who questions the personal interference of God in answer to the call of his children. But there was another phase of the history of that campaign which seems to be absolutely unaccountable on any other hypothesis but the direct and special interference of superhuman intelligence.

The number seven! It is called "a sacred number"; but why it has been credited with its peculiar significance is, perhaps, the effect of its mention so often in the Bible. The various theories, reasonable and fanciful, for the sacredness of the number seven need not be rehearsed in a record of simple facts like these which this account preserves. But the daily appearance of the number seven in the evangelistic history of the Grace Church through the five years and two months before the large Temple was completed has never been explained by any solution other than by accrediting it to some power or law above the normal. The "five years' meetings" were only the usual meetings of the small church and no evangelistic or unusual endeavors were used, nor were any special methods tried. Evangelists of noted power sometimes addressed the church or gave sermons at the church in connection with some convention or association, but none of those instrumentalities seemed to affect the answers to the prayers of the people. The church sessions were simple, practical, social, and fully democratic, but the prayers were full of faith and feeling and were brief and direct.

One evening, in a meeting held in a small basement room, there were seven young people, strangers to one another, who arrived as newcomers. Each one stated that he had come under a strange and

15

irresistible impulse unaccountable to him. Each asked the people to pray for his soul. That was the opening of the continuous stream of seven new converts each week for five years. That repetition of the number seven was not especially noticed until it had been repeated through several weeks. Then the people began to expect it, and during the active enterprises connected with the building of the new Temple it had a powerful effect on the courage and faith of that small company.

As the years came and went with no change in that weekly number of fresh seekers after God, a feeling of awe held the worshipers to such an extent that when the seventh man or woman arose to come forward a deep sigh passed through the congregation. Sometimes the leader of the meeting paused or asked for "the hesitating one" if the full number did not at first appear. But there was no prearrangement and no attempt or purpose to cease the arrival of newcomers after the number seven had been reached. The church was too deeply impressed with the seeming miracle to undertake any experiments with it.

Continual prayer was all that was attempted. People ceased to ask their acquaintances to come to the meetings, and the usual revival methods were omitted. Real prayer, sincere singing, and a short comment on some verse of Scripture made up the usual order of services, aside from the regular preaching on Sunday. Various explanations of this mysterious and systematic manifestation of some hidden spiritual force have been advanced by students of the unusual occurrence. Some undevout friends have rested satisfied with the belief that it was only a coincidence or an accidental repetition of a natural phenomenon. The skeptic said that there was no mystery about it, as it merely "happened so". Others, more devout, declared that the people must have habitually "let go of their faith" when seven appeared, and that according to their faith "was the limitation of the numbers." Others believed that it must have been, consciously or unconsciously, arranged by persons managing the meeting, and not a few outsiders regarded the statement of the facts as a clear falsehood. They said it could not have been possible, and that there was surely some deception in the arrangements or reports. But the hundreds of intelligent and conscientious people who were present week after week became fully satisfied that it was the work of the Divine Spirit sent in answer to their prayers. Some of the circumstances connected with that large accession to the church will be of interest to the student.

During the years when the building was being constructed many simple schemes were devised by the people to raise money for the work. But prayer was a part of every endeavor. Fairs, suppers, and concerts were often used to raise funds, and, although a worldly spirit often creeps into church entertainments, there came there a devotional spirit which seemed to transfigure every work. The devotional meetings held in a side hall when the church fairs were going on at the Academy of Music in Philadelphia ever had the same startling result - the unchangeable number, seven newcomers, came out. One evening a specially large number of citizens were at a dinner given to arrange plans for securing the money for the first payment to the contractor who was laying the foundation for the Temple. A visitor, in his speech, said that he had been more interested in the "steady revival," of which he had heard, than in the feast, and that he was quite disappointed to learn that for the first time in three years the church had omitted its weekly prayer meeting to give place to a dinner. Thereupon, Deacon Stoddard, a devout man, arose and suggested that before the guests left the table the presiding officer should give the usual invitation for anyone to arise and declare his decision to follow God. After several eloquent and entertaining speeches on general topics the invitation was given for the religious confession, and, to the amazement of many, just seven young men arose.

A deep, spiritual emotion filled the hearts of all present. In two or three instances the number was less than seven who responded before the benediction was pronounced, and some said, "The spell is broken." But in all cases another seeker after God appeared before the people left the room. In several instances persons were too much overcome or too timid to stand out before a public meeting, and they persuaded someone sitting near them to get up and ask prayers for them. But there was no prolongation of any service and no outlay of money for exhorters or singers. Naturally that remarkable condition attracted a throng of people, and before the Temple was opened the church and Sunday-school rooms at Mervine and Berks streets were crowded beyond endurance.

At the first great prayer meeting held in the Temple, when the call was made for converts the number who came forward was seventy-seven. From that time (1892) there has been no resumption of a regular number of seekers. Often the number seven, seventy-seven, forty-nine, and seventy appear in the number of those who arose for prayer or in the list of those who were received at the same time into the church. At one Easter service two hundred and seventy-seven were baptized. But those "five years' revivals" stand out as five most beautiful years in the memory of the thousands still living who recall them.

All of that company of believers prayed, and on those stormy days when the curious crowd were kept away the people drew together in sincere devotion, and the most dreary days without were the most happy within. God seemed more reachable and the domestic sweetness of the church home was much more fully appreciated when the snow shadowed the panes, when the wild storms beat on the doors, and when only earnest worshipers ventured out to church.

For more than fifteen years three thousand tickets of admission to the regular church services were taken up several days in advance, and when a very stormy day kept many ticket holders away special and repeated prayer was made especially for them. The effect of those stormy days of special prayer was one of the most remarkable experiences of the church life. Letters came in great numbers from different parts of the world, saying that they missed the services, but felt decidedly impressed to send for some needed information or for special religious advice.

Many cathedrals, churches, homes, and charity halls have been built on prayer and faith, so that the construction of the Baptist Temple, on a prominent corner of Philadelphia's widest street, in the heart of the city, by a few poor people, may not seem strange. Yet the fact that God has prospered other enterprises is only a confirmation of the theory that God answered the prayers of Grace Church in giving providential assistance in the construction of the Temple.

When the church voted to go on and pay for the lot and build a church to seat over three thousand in the upper auditorium and two thousand in the lower hall, there was no money in hand or pledged. Yet there was no recklessness, no tempting God in their faith. When the contracts were entered into with the builder, or the furniture manufacturer, provision was made carefully for any contingency. If for any unforeseen reason the great building had been unfinished at any stage of construction, all bills would have been paid. But each advance in the work was made after special prayer over each division of the building enterprise. The foundation was constructed after special prayer, then came the walls, the roof, the carpenter's inside work, the painting, the furniture, and the organ - each being the object of prayerful consideration.

There were a few instances, however, which are worthy of special mention. There was a point when the contract for the stone for the walls was held up by the quarry proprietors, as they feared to venture on so large a job with no guaranty but a mechanic's right of lien. At that time a new savings bank was opened at Columbia Avenue, two squares from the Temple, and President Cummings, head of the bank, offered to assist the church in any safe way. How he came to know of the proposed work, or what special reason he had for helping a people with whom he was not personally acquainted, was never explained. But he was a noble citizen. His influence was itself a powerful aid in all the business of the church.

One day a stranger (General Wagner, president of the Third National Bank) was driving by the half-constructed church when an "impulse" seized him to go into the building under construction. He was a Presbyterian elder and a stranger to all the members of Grace Church. He was a great man of business, a person of unflinching integrity whose coolness in emergencies and whose conservative management of financial institutions made him a trusted authority for private, for city, or for national finances. In a few words of conversation with the contractor in the building General Wagner was told that the church was being built "by faith in prayer." He told General Wagner that thus far "every payment had been made promptly, with nothing left over." From that hour the general was a strong, unmovable friend and backer of the Temple enterprise. The Tenth National Bank and its offspring, the Columbia Trust Company, and the Third National Bank, of which General Wagner was president, were ever safely used as a reference, and often tens of thousands of dollars were loaned by them to the church for short periods. The trustees and the deacons of the church were prayerful men of stable common sense and successful in their own labor or business. There was no foolish overpiousness, no loud professions of religious fervor, but a determined trust in God's promise to heed the call of those who loved him.

Mr. John Little, a Quaker by inheritance and training, was a leading mind in the affairs of the church and was for many years the treasurer of the Temple University. He was a quiet, keenly modest man, but living a transparent truthfulness and honesty which commanded the confidence of all who knew him and secured for him a love that can never die. He said that he had two special places for prayer, one being in the Temple and the other on the street. Mr. Charles F. Stone (whose wife, Mrs. Maria L. Stone, continued his work after he died) was the treasurer of the church at the critical period and was a man endowed with excellent business ability and a devout man full of good works. He, too, had a "good name" which was rather to be chosen as a financial recommendation than great riches. These men are not mentioned because of their special claim to attention above the others associated with them, but simply as two specimens of the prayer-making company who moved on unhesitatingly, yet carefully, in doing the thing which many declared could not be done. The weekly reports from the committees and individuals showing how God had raised up, unexpectedly or strangely, friends of the undertaking, often caused a deep feeling of awe and sent the people out with fresh determination to work cheerfully on.

A single instance of the many hundreds reported will probably answer the inquiries of others now engaged in some like work. Looking back upon the incident after thirty years the plan or the purpose of the divine leadership, so hidden then, becomes reasonable and clear. Why the Lord wished to use only three hundred men out of Gideon's great army was not understood at the time, but all can see now that the purpose was to bring the Lord's hand into vision and win for him the recognition which would have gone to the human army.

Only once did the people of the Temple falter and their prayers seem ineffective. Only once did those Philadelphia worshipers limit their faith. But that one period of doubt came when the question was suddenly thrust before the church whether they would try to put in a suitable church organ. Many claimed that they had reached the utmost limit of sacrifice. Some said that the church ought to be fully satisfied if they could buy seats for the first services. Others strongly declared that after all the asking of God and man for aid to build the Temple they could not expect either God or man to help them to buy an unnecessary organ. Through thirty-eight years the church has never had any quarrel to settle in all its history, and that division of opinion did not assume an angry or excited phase. It was simply a feeling in some of the people that the Lord had done wonders and that, now that the church was out of the wilderness, it was full time to let the people and God's providence rest.

When the question arose whether the church should venture to purchase a suitable church organ it was decided by a large majority that it could not be undertaken. The small minority were Gideon's three hundred. One member of that small body asked the church for the privilege of putting in the organ, "if he could raise all of the ten thousand dollars needed without asking a contribution from anyone who had already given or subscribed toward the building." Even that conservative offer was accepted by a reluctant and small majority.

Then that member began a downright, heart-stretching wrestle with the Angel of God. He spent two successive nights in the Temple in hard and tearful prayer. He had nothing to give. He must secure the whole from others. He pleaded with God to let him work with Him in awakening the hearts of possible givers. But the Lord was not willing to give to man the major part of the glory of success. The murmuring people must be made ashamed of their lack of faith in the Lord who had safely led them thus far. The contract for the organ was made with a company whose agent said they usually sold their organs on faith, but that churches always paid .the cost and often paid in advance of the date when the notes matured. The purchaser of the Temple organ did not feel authorized to put in the organ with no money in hand, at least for the first installment on the price to be paid. But all the men he approached refused to give because it was "overdoing it," and was "too improbable" for credence or assistance.

But the purchaser did not waver. The time set for the payment of the first fifteen hundred dollars came. The note the purchaser gave was due on Monday. The debtor had asked the Sunday-morning prayer meeting to remember him especially "on the morrow." He had until three o'clock Monday to raise the money to save his note from protest. He had written to a relative to ask for a loan of fifteen hundred dollars, but the letter had not been sent to the mailbox. When he entered his room just before church services a working girl who was a member of the church came quietly to his door and handed him a letter in which, when he opened it, he found a check for fifteen hundred dollars. The letter and check were signed by a laboring man in Massilon, Ohio, who wrote that he had not been asked to give anything, but he had heard that the church "hoped soon to get an organ." He felt impressed to send this check and to ask the church to accept it on the condition that, should he ever be reduced to actual need, the church should endeavor to aid him in some way.

The second payment due came as an unexpected draft from Boston for five hundred dollars, which must be honored or refused within three days. But in the same mail with the notice of the draft came two money orders from the executor of an estate in California, saying that the deceased testator had left the distribution of certain sums to the discretion of the executor and he had decided to send five hundred dollars toward "the music in the new Temple."

The third payment was met by funds raised by solicitation, about which there seemed to be nothing remarkable. Other payments were made by gifts clearly sent in connection with the appeal of the believer, but the last payment was the most unaccountable of all. Three one-hundred-dollar bills were pushed under the door of the church study by some one never discovered, and a certificate of mining stock worth seven hundred dollars was sent from Butte, Montana, without other signature except that on the face of the certificate. The blank for the purchaser of the stock was blank. Public efforts were made to find the givers, but without success. Well might the people feel that the voice of the organ was the voice of God.

When the organ was dedicated and Dr. D. D. Wood led the devotion with inspired fingers and sightless eyes the church congregation was a beautiful sight - like a sea sparkling with tears. When the great chorus was singing the hymn, "God moves in a mysterious way his wonders to perform," a large number of the singers were so choked with emotion that they ceased to sing and Doctor Wood said the event was one of the most thrilling in all his experiences with choirs.

These are "the simple annals of the poor," but they illustrate and inculcate great principles which are applicable to any work for the Lord.

Chapter III - Healing the Sick

THE health and happiness of mankind depend in a great degree on faith. Every emotion of the body and every action of the mind is an exhibition of faith. Persons who believe they are well, even if they are ill, will soon recover, and persons who believe that they will not be sick are seldom ill. There is no department of human life so dependent on belief as that connected with health. Millions would arise, take up their couches and walk, if they could be made to believe that they could do so. To believe a falsehood has cured many people, and consciences waver between the duty to tell a patient the clear truth when he is very ill and to make him believe a lie in order that he may get well.

It must also be stated, in fidelity to the truth, that the subject of healing by faith has called out a host of the half-insane classes who proclaim with trumpet tones some cases of divine healing which are unworthy of a moment's consideration. Hence, out of a collection of possibly sincere letters, many have been rejected altogether as foolish or misleading. Eleven hundred written testimonies to cases of healing in direct answer to prayer at the Baptist Temple have been carefully examined and the trustworthy testimonies tabulated. Those "years of healing" to which reference is so often made were years of prayer and years of faith. After deducting all the questionable cases, and after a wide allowance for the naturally health-giving and health-preserving power, the normal human belief is that there remains an overwhelmingly convincing amount of evidence that healing is directly brought about by sincere prayer.

Through several years cases were reported to the church or pastors which convinced all who knew the people and the circumstances that some intelligent power, higher than human knowledge, had interfered to heal the sick. But when the knowledge of those trustworthy cases came to be known, and especially when they had awakened much excited comment, then the "cranks" and monomaniacs crowded to the front and vociferously proclaimed the most absurd miracles, to the disgust of reasonable men and women and greatly to the damage of the beneficent work.

Sometimes all references to healing were omitted in the pulpit and shut out from the meetings for prayer until the wild advocates of divine healing settled down and dispassionate views could be taken. Many intelligent devout men repudiated the whole experiment, believing that the excitement over it was doing much more harm than good. But the larger part who saw the people who had been cured by the unexplainable means were steadfast and went on sincerely thanking God for his wonderful works among the children of men.

A digest of the written testimonies showed that cataracts had unrolled without the touch of a surgeon's knife, although the greatest number of the restoration of sight to the blind were with the aid of apparent means. The methods by which the Lord restored their sight did not make their gratitude to him for restoration any the less commendable. Mysterious and evidently dangerous internal tumors disappeared slowly or suddenly in a manner unexplainable by the most learned physicians.

By far the greatest number of the eleven hundred cases selected for consideration out of the multitude of testimonies were cases in some way directly connected with the nervous system. Patients long confined in an insane asylum were brought home and cured of what had been considered hopeless insanity. There were many cases of various forms of brain diseases, while in all these cases a specially conservative examiner could declare that they might have been cured by the special or wise treatment.

Yet, even if such were the case, the devout man who prayed may claim that the treatment was only a part of God's healing plan. It was often declared publicly and without any contradiction that for long seasons there was not one person ill in bed in the more than one thousand homes represented in the membership of the church worshiping in the Temple. Usually health reigned in the entire church, and it was reasonably claimed that in five years more than six hundred cases of lung and throat trouble were permanently healed. Epidemics afflicted the city, and, quoting Doctor Haehnlen, it was declared that "the Angel of Death had passed over the congregation, taking none. Of course the people believed that if they went to the Temple to pray for the recovery of their friends they would surely be favorably answered. Many have, however, written that if that condition of faith could be secured in the doctor, nurse, and family, that spirit of hope would be naturally aroused in the patient and aid greatly in the recovery.

But the men who pray can say with greater confidence that in every case it was, at least, God working with man. At all events, the general health of the congregation must be far better than would have been the case with the same people if they had not gone to church and prayed.

Hundreds of men and women live on in health and vigor who were in that congregation at middle age thirty-five years ago. Their strength "is not abated," although some of them were invalids thirty years ago. The healing force of a cheerful faith is everywhere acknowledged to be a health-preserving agency of vital importance in the establishment of public health. It is a vital necessity in thousands of individual cases. Such a condition is probably often a gift of God - through the influence of his suggesting and soothing spirit.

Even the most ultra-conservative critic at the Temple who tried hard to see in these many cases of restoration only the "working out of some natural law" confessed that if his child was sick he "would not dare to omit praying" for its recovery. The conclusion of the whole matter is in the settled conviction in the minds of nearly all the worshipers at the Temple that God does answer prayer for the sick.

Chapter IV - Prayer for the Home

ONE Sunday evening at the usual services the invitation was given, as is customary, for such persons who especially desired to be mentioned in the daily prayers of the people to rise for a moment before the singing of the last hymn. The sermon had not mentioned the need of prayer and contained no special evangelistic appeal. The invitation was the customary proceeding throughout the year. The three thousand seats were all filled. The audience was composed, as usual, largely of men, and they were men of middle age. There were young people, representing both sexes, scattered through the audience, and lines of them along the back rows of seats in the distant gallery. No attempt was made to emphasize the ordinary invitation in any special manner.

But when the solemn moment came for the prayer-seekers to rise, the response was so general that the preacher asked those who had risen to remain standing until the pastors could see them and count them. There were over five hundred, and for a few weeks that was about the usual number of those who arose.

But the preacher was especially startled by the fact which he had not especially noted on previous occasions: that the majority of those who asked for prayer were young people. The scene, when those youthful faces appeared on every side and in so large a congregation, filled the soul of the beholder with almost painful awe. It led the preacher to meditate a moment to ask God and himself why so many young people took such a solemn, sincere interest in prayer at that time. The thought led him, before the benediction, to request all who had stood forth for prayer to write to him a personal and confidential letter explaining why they desired to be mentioned in the prayers of the people.

The letters came the next week by the hundred. It was an astonishing revelation. The letters from unmarried people were culled out of the collection and reread at leisure. Some of them were in need of higher wages; some were seeking for a personal religious awakening; some asked prayers for friends, for business, for safe journey, for health, or for other protection and relief. But out of two hundred and eighty-seven letters from those young people, over two hundred mentioned - directly or indirectly - their strong desire for a husband, a wife, or a home.

The details of lovers' quarrels were opened up, the anguish of broken engagements expressed on tear-stained sheets of note paper, and many doubtful lovers wished the Lord would reveal to them whether their choice had been a wise one or whether their love was deep enough for such an extremely important matter as marriage. The letters revealed such a general longing for a home that one seldom realizes is really existent. There were a few letters from young college women and university men, but the greater portion were from working girls. They were the most touchingly sacred records of the everyday thoughts of young women, all sincerely and modestly expressed. When those young women saw some handsomely gowned wife pass her desk, her counter, her bench, or loom, leading a bright-faced little son, the working girl's soul uttered an unvoiced shriek for a home, for a noble husband's protection, and for children of her own. Women waiters who daily fed the wives of wealthy merchants or of prosperous manufacturers wrote how terrible was the thought that they were going to be homeless and penniless in their old age - one great prayer going up to high heaven for holy domestic love and a place they could call "home".

After that evening's call upon the seekers after God to rise, the request for letters was repeated. The answers which came even into thousands revealed the general request for the leadership of the Spirit of the all-wise God in directing the all-important affairs of the heart. Some letters detailed the horrors of broken hearts; some revealed dark sins; and some told of betrayal or of base and traitorous ingratitude. But the majority were letters from lonely but upright women of high ideals and of noble life. Some of the communications were from conscientious young men asking God's help in deciding their choice or for the influence of God in their favor when their chosen one should make up her hesitating mind. Some were calls for forgiveness and for human advice in most complicated cases where the writer had been misunderstood or where he had thoughtlessly made a promise he must recall.

All wanted a home. The honest souls standing out in the open before God, where the restraints of human custom and the reluctance of a pure modesty were, for the moment, overcome, wrote out the sincerest prayer of all. Their soul's need was a home.

Of all the holy ambitions of a normal man or woman the purpose to have a home is the highest. A home on earth and a home in heaven constitute the soul's chiefest need. Around that transfigured word gather all that is highest and purest in human thinking and all that is most sacred and heavenly in human feeling, In the beginning the Almighty created man - "Male and female created he them." The first home was in Paradise. The last home will be there.

He who has an income to maintain a house, who has an intelligent, unselfish wife, who can look about his table and see children with clear intellects and loving hearts, is conspicuously foolish if he does not see that he already has the best the world can give.
She who can cast off all anxiety for maintenance and can devote herself to the care and training of her own little ones, and who can respect and deeply love her chosen mate, has God's best gifts already in her possession. Gratitude to the heavenly Father will lead such recipients of his richest bounty to forget not to aid those who have less. Nothing on earth of wealth, applause, or mundane wisdom can equal, in the least measure, the temporal and eternal values of a real home. Therefore it is wise and the mark of a godly character to pray heartily for a husband, or for a wife, or for children.

A reasonable valuation of such domestic treasures makes a hideous crime of every violation of the laws and customs which make a loving home possible. Profanity of speech, theft of money, or traitorous breaking of any other contract is a light sin compared with the brutal sins of the libertine or the unchastity of the woman who sells herself, or who, with evil intent, entices a man to home-breaking crime. So important is this matter that it is the fit subject for constant prayer for those who have not chosen to be a martyr or decided to give up all on earth for a home in heaven. And, even in the latter case, the call to take up any work inconsistent with the maintenance of a home should be overwhelmingly emphatic to command obedience.

Hence, those appeals to Heaven for domestic rest of soul were all normal and all of supreme importance. When that great collection of letters were each answered, the reply contained a counter-request for a report in due season which should state when and how the prayer for a home had been answered. Those reports have also been carefully tabulated. But here again the critical adherent to the theory concerning the unchangeable laws of nature tries to escape any committal to religious dogmas by claiming that the mating instinct is an inborn sentiment common to fishes, beasts, and birds, and that mankind mates by accidental acquaintanceship or by the pressure of necessity or ungoverned passion. Such arguments convince many people who deride the claim that marriages are "made in heaven". But after every such theory is suggested and analyzed, after every allowance for the outworking of "natural selection," there is left an important place for the intrusion or domination of a superhuman power. To that fact, the simple, unvarnished tale of the experience of the years at the Temple bear eloquent testimony.

A book of this character requires that out of the many reports only the most representative cases should be selected, and that the mention should be as brief as is consistent with clearness. The number of marriages which every church, small or great, brings about is ever the astonishment of any preacher who goes back over the history of forty years of church life. The church in any community is a center of more or less of social life and furnishes an opportunity for the best young people to meet on a plane of safe association. The married people, and especially the owners of homes, are the very best people in any town or city. As a rule, all people possessed of religious character marry. The unmarried masses of the people, or those who are most often unhappily mated, are often the unstable classes who are not closely bound to moral principles. Religious life and home life are twin sisters. They belong to the same family and have the same likes, dislikes, and motives. They are congenial and necessary companions almost everywhere.

Let us examine the leading events wherein we seem to recognize the divine hand and which led directly to the setting up of religious homes. One lady clerk in a department store, in her first letter asking for prayer, said that she was forty-one years of age and that she had been twenty years in the store. She said that she had hoped for a home all her adult life, but had abandoned the hope and wished only to die soon. She asked if suicide would be wrong under such sad circumstances. The following Sabbath morning, after the service, the pastor of her church incidentally introduced her to a widower of her age who had a comfortable house, but who had rented it because he had no children. The widower asked the pastor a few days later to pray for him as he had a "very important matter" on his mind.

Several days later he came to the minister and said that he had dreamed three times and in each dream he had precisely the same experience. He dreamed that he was climbing a steep hill in Bethlehem, Pennsylvania, and he had called for help to a lady standing above him near the path, and when he took her hand he recognized her as the lady to whom the minister had introduced him. He declared that he really wished to set up a home again, but his first impression of that lady was decidedly unfavorable. The minister unreservedly advised the widower never to let a mere dream influence him to overcome his calm judgment. The minister said that dreams were often contrary to fair reasoning and should not be consulted in such important matters.

A few days later the lady called on the minister to ask him if there was "any truth in dreams." Then she greatly surprised the minister by saying that she dreamed several times that she was on a steep bank near a cousin's home in Bethlehem, Pennsylvania, and as the earth began dangerously to break beneath her feet a man caught her and supported her to the safe path. The mysterious thing in her story was that she recognized the man as
the gentleman to whom she had been introduced that Sunday morning, but whose name she had forgotten. She said that the

repetition of the dream "set her to thinking," and she had called to inquire who the gentleman was and what trust could be placed in dreams. The minister was too surprised to declare again that no faith could be put in any dreams. The minister said nothing to her about his previous interview with the widower and let her depart with the remark that if the Lord intended she should marry that man, the Lord would also speak to the man about it in some clear manner. The Lord never advises one party to enter into such a contract when he knows the other party is unwilling. In every holy marriage both parties are equally inspired with the spirit of God and are both absolutely convinced that the Lord had brought them together.

The minister soon wrote to the widower, advising him to call on the lady and tell her frankly that he desired to make her acquaintance with a view to a marriage, if both should be satisfied that it would be right. Every reader of this incident recognizes or feels the impression of the universal law of nature and can prophesy safely that they would marry. The minister was not present at the wedding, but he was informed by those who did attend the ceremony that the bridegroom told the guests the history of their dreams and claimed that they were "obeying the voice of God" when they arranged for that marriage.

The doubting persons who claim that the repetition of the dreams and the accidental meetings were singular coincidences that were in no way influenced by angel spirits, do have enough support to make the angel theory one of faith and remove the claim from the class of "scientific demonstrations." The facts related cannot be questioned. But the conclusions from those facts may differ widely and still be more or less reasonable.

The mysterious attraction which leads the bird and the beast to choose their mates is of the same nature as that mating instinct which prevails universally among mankind. But man's reasoning power and his self-control make his choice of a wife a far more complicated matter. The healthiest, strongest, and most intellectual races are ever those whose laws and customs allow the greatest opportunity for unprejudiced choice in the selection of life mates. Intermarriage of family relations, or the marriages within a narrow circle of the same race, ever produce weaklings and often idiots. In the lands where the parents arrange all the marriages there is but little progress and but few real homes. Wherever the parties refuse to be guided by the higher law of affinity, or by a recognition of Divine Providence, there will seldom be found a real home. "Affinity" is an abused word, and is often used to bolster up a bad cause or to excuse a cruel crime. But the close student of anthropology ever finds that the known natural laws do not account for every case, nor can a satisfactory solution of sex attraction in human affairs be found without admitting the mysterious and potent force that is only spiritual.

Looking back over the marriage records of the Baptist Temple for thirty years, there appear some significant facts concerning homemaking by prayer. Through those thirty years of the record-keeping there was an average of sixteen marriages a month, or five thousand and one hundred in thirty years. The same pastor who officiated at the marriage of the parents also, in many cases, officiated at the weddings of the children. Not one case of divorce can be discovered and only two cases of estrangement. The records of many praying churches probably show the same conditions.

But it is a sublime, soul-satisfying thing to meditate on such a great list of happy homes. The searcher, when he notes the birthplaces of bride and groom, finds that they often come from the most distant places and represent nearly all the races of the world. Calcutta united with New York, Iceland with New Orleans, Philadelphia with Chicago, Quebec with Quakertown, Worcester (Massachusetts) with Camden (New Jersey), Japan with Chester (Pennsylvania), Alaska with Columbia (South Carolina), country villages with cities, obscure daughters of prairie farmers with sailors on the Atlantic, millionaires' sons with working girls, and thousands of members of the church of all adult ages uniting with other members of whom they knew nothing in childhood.

From the atheist's point of view he can see nothing in that history but a jumble of accidents or a snarl of events which cannot be untangled. But to the devout believer in the theory that God sends his angels to arrange the homemaking as he did in the case of Rebecca and Isaac, that list of homes presents a sublime view of a system for the kind distribution of Heaven's chiefest blessings. Out of the seventy-two hundred who united with Grace Church and its missions in the thirty years mentioned above, all but twenty-nine have been married. As a homemaking-agency in the history of our nation the churches must hold the leading place.

When the remarkable series of reported dreams became known and was being discussed by the people, there arose many men and women with unbalanced minds who testified to the most inconsistent miracles in connection with their dreams. Among the letters which they sent in when testimonials were called for, there were nearly one hundred which related foolish and impossible experiences and which made the whole debate ridiculous. But that uprising of those who were "possessed of evil spirits" did not prove that the one case so well established was not the work of an angel of God. There may be ten thousand dreams which are of no special value and which are caused by natural law. But God seems to use only one here and there for his special purposes.

Thousands of seeds fall on the earth, but only one may be selected to grow. There were cases related where dreams were specially potent to the dreamers because of the suggestions made by the dreams to the waking minds. A dream is often very potent as a reminder, or as a caution, and is often a providential event used in God's plan, although the dreams in themselves may have nothing unusual about them. There could be no clearly remembered dream which did not have some effect on the thought and later actions of the dreamer. With that view many dreams need not have their origin in a special visit of an angel of God.

But again we must believe that there are dreams in which the angel of God appears to man directly, and that such dreams are possible in any age of the human world. Each claim, therefore, to a revelation of

God in a dream should stand alone and be accepted or rejected after a careful study of all the causes and effects.

The experiences with the Holy Spirit during those years of constant prayer should find a special place in this record. For there were devout souls who seemed to be constantly filled with the divine sense, and they surely enjoyed the peace of God which passeth all understanding. Here, again, we walk near a line that cannot exactly be located and enjoy emotions or inspirations which cannot be described. An all-pervading joy illumined every part of the human soul.

"Where are you going so early this Sunday morning?" was often asked of the hastening pedestrian, and it was a common experience to hear him reply, "I am going to the morning prayer meeting in the Temple to meet the Holy Spirit." The Holy Spirit was there awaiting him. There were Pentecostal days - supreme hours of strange elation, seasons of heavenly bliss which cannot be accounted for on any psychological basis. A holy brooding of a sin-expelling spiritual atmosphere permeated by a power like a perfume.

It was an indwelling of the Spirit which carried a purifying fumigation wherein the worshiper simply let go of himself and rested in the arms of his heavenly Father. Many felt that sacred presence and could only express themselves in tears. Such Pentecostal visitations of the Spirit have doubtless come to thousands of churches and to millions of worshipers in other places, and this experience at the Temple is not mentioned as if it were an unusual thing where prayer is the habit of all the people. But it confirms the history of the visits of the Holy Spirit related in the Bible, and must be accepted as a proof of the fact that there is communication between the spirit world and the world in which we live in the flesh.

Chapter V - Prayer and the Bible

THERE are three methods used distinctively in the study of the Bible and upon each of them prayer has a clear effect. This fact comes out fully in the written testimonials received from the members of the church worshiping in the Baptist Temple. One individual may read the Bible as he would read any other book, and, consequently, finds it dull reading. Another studies the historical references as an archeologist or as the scientific specialists examine a rare specimen. To them it is a curious and strange collection of ancient manuscripts, and such a student finds amusement in the research. Another regards the Book as a miraculous revelation from God, and he handles the volume with reverent care and reads the statements it contains as he would a letter sent from heaven direct to him. Those three classes are found in almost every religious gathering, and it is an intensely interesting thing to observe at close range the various effects of prayer on such a congregation.

When the leader of the prayer service approaches the Bible with the manner of a delighted seeker after truth, and, before opening the Book, leads the people in a direct appeal to the Divine Spirit for instruction and inspiration, the interest of the worshipers in the Book is especially awakened. When the leader prays fervently and with frank sincerity that the passages of the Bible to be read shall be illumined or be made alive with special meaning and new emphasis, then the Book will be an interesting volume to nearly all of the gathering. And when the leader is himself expecting a special revelation from that Book at that time, his personal magnetism combines with his manner to help the worshiper into a receptive, expectant state of mind. The people then expect to hear "an important message from a most important person."

The helpfulness of those conditions anyone would understand, as they are in accord with human experience in other gatherings. But the effect of the prayer in bringing to each person present a different message from the same verse puts the matter over into the realm of the supernatural.

At one prayer meeting at the Temple, when a severe storm had cut down the attendance to a number under twenty, the prayerful attitude of all present made the session one of special spiritual illumination. The Scriptures were read with accuracy and natural emphasis, and then each listener was requested to state informally what was the chief lesson which the reading brought to him. Each person present received a distinct and helpful suggestion differing from the suggestions made to any of the others. It is that well-established fact, so often experienced, that makes the Bible a book unlike any other. In this, too, is shown the importance of persuading everyone to read the Bible for and by himself.

It seems, however, to be universally true that when the Bible is prayerfully, intelligently read aloud each praying listener receives some message of special importance to himself. While all that evening heard the same words from the same mouth, yet the circumstances of each life were different from every other; the experiences had been unlike, the inherited dispositions were different, the meaning of the words was shaded by the variation in their home use, and a full allowance was freely made for those differing effects. But those considerations cannot, to the calm, critical student of the inspiration of the Bible, account for the special and mysterious messages which come to each participant in the meeting. The suggestions are often beyond the application of the law of "the association of ideas." They cannot be explained by any of the known psychological laws which seem generally to govern the human mind. This experience with the Bible is the best evidence of its divine inspiration. Archeological, psychological, etymological, or historical analysis cannot establish the accuracy of the Bible so surely as that actual experience.

The best proof is subjective. The secular argument that the Bible carries on its face the evidence that the writers were all inspired by a "good motive" is surely an excellent reason for believing the Bible to be "inspired." A holy motive, apparent in its wise communications, is clearly shown in the Bible. The etymologist who rests his case on the conclusion that the words "inspired by God " were formerly written "inspired by the Good," and that the "All Good" being is the ideal God, is not far from the safe definition. That does not in any way conflict with the theory that "all Scripture, inspired by the 'All Good,' is profitable for doctrine, for reproof, for correction, for instruction in righteousness." The complications into which the narrow theologian or technical philosopher falls when attempting to reason about the Almighty often make the study bewildering and unprofitable. The testimony of the good and great through all the ages that every line of the Book is written with the unselfish purpose to do good is sufficient warrant for the common reader in concluding that it has some unusual inspiration.

The question was often discussed at the Temple whether it was safe after prayer to open the Bible at random and be guided by the first verse on which the eye rested. Some claimed that it was always safe to trust it. Others said that it was only occasionally that they found it to be reasonably instructive. Still others believed that the ascribing of such magic, or miraculous, power to the Book was clearly a form of forbidden idolatry. But the majority of the praying Bible readers felt convinced that the selection of texts at random could not be trusted. Yet here again we find strong evidence that sometimes the worshiper is directed to a particular record which seems to be selected by a divine mind.

Again, it is wholly a matter of faith. The boy who asked his father for a silver dollar and found one in the road which some traveler had accidentally dropped, concluded that there was no design on the part of his father to give him the dollar. But when he found a dollar there the third time, his conclusion that his father had placed all three of the dollars there for him was not unreasonable, but, nevertheless, erroneous.

So while the Lord surely has established certain laws or customs which seem permanent, yet he has the power and may change the laws or allow exceptions, and one cannot believe in prayer without believing that such changes are sometimes made. It is a far greater strain upon human credulity not to believe it than it is to believe it. The careful use of common sense in the interpretation of Biblical or unusual events, examples, and records of wisdom is ever the safe and sane proceeding. If one should pray for divine direction and opened the Bible at random to find the Lord's advice he should always examine the verse to see if its teaching or direction accorded with his petition.

In a "call" to the ministry there must be a conviction of duty in the soul and also a road providentially opened to the would-be laborer. So in all the thousands of answers to prayer at the Temple there was found a conjunction of circumstances which showed that the worker was called by the same Lord who had a work to be done. The will of man is a strong force and is in itself an effectual, fervent prayer. The Lord prospers the person whose righteous will is decided, persistent, and uncompromising.

The too-frequent consultation of Bible texts for hints or for direction shows a habit of doubt which is often a clear evidence of weakness. But in this, as in almost every other experiment, it is the consensus of opinion that the Lord does often inspire the Bible, especially for certain devout seekers, and that he inspires the soul with a keen, sensitive apprehension and appreciation of the special revelation. The spiritually minded man or woman is the only one who can interpret a spiritual book.

The chief value of the Bible is as a spiritual guide. It is the only book which explains the Creator's revelation to this world, and is the only one which gives a trustworthy description of the spiritual world. What a shadow would pass over the earth, and what destruction, devastation, and misery would be experienced, if, in one moment, all knowledge of the Bible were crossed out!

Sane men who reverently pray for the inspiration when they read the Scriptures are the only safe guides to its sacred meaning. All who came to the Temple to pray seem to have been lead to the Bible at once, and thousands have learned to love it. To those who have prayed long over it, it has become a continual feast.

Chapter VI - Spiritual Telepathy

IT would be no more surprising for the discovery of a means of direct spirit communication with the spiritual life than it was to be convinced that Marconi had discovered a sure method of telegraphing and telephoning without wires. The discovery of the laws which made electricity a servant of mankind was an astonishing revelation which was as unbelievable as is the law of spiritual telepathy. Human telepathy, which is a mysterious means of communication between persons without the use of known material agency, is in the initial and experimental stage. But the possibility of such thought transference is generally admitted. The psychical researchers into that science should be encouraged in every way.

On the eve of every such advance in human achievement there always appear a host of superstitious dreamers and wild prophets, even in the study of science, who hinder the sane searcher and often becloud the mind of the student who is on the direct road to the needed discovery.

Spiritualism, which is here used as a comprehensive term, frequently confuses the deliberations of honest truth-seekers with the advertised works of deceivers, but it includes much in its curriculum that is worth careful study. Among the host of disordered or weak minds who claim so much that is foolish in connection with spiritual revelations, there are a respectable number of thoughtful, conservative searchers who cannot be easily deceived. In all the successful "isms " in a civilization, and in all the popular religious sects, there is ever some basic truth. Some one idea is so true and so strongly emphasized that it often carries along a backbreaking load of absurd theories. The thoughtless throng hears of several well-authenticated cases of fraud, or of absurd teaching, in connection with spiritual meetings, or messages, and leaps to the conviction that all claims of so-called spiritualists are not worthy of consideration. So many thousands have tried so sincerely to recall their dead without the least sign of an answer that they refuse to examine the testimony of great men, like Sir Oliver Lodge, whose belief differs from their belief. They will not read what great minds have expressed on the subject. But the great discoveries recently made in materialistic sciences have led thoughtful men to hope for great discoveries in the relation of this existence to another life. This expectation, or strong hope, made the study of the spiritual revelations and conditions at the Temple a most thrilling occupation.

The reports of the answers to prayer so often use the words "happened to think" that the observer cannot escape the conviction that either the living human mind does send spirit messages or that some mysterious power acts for it in forwarding messages. The great list of mysterious impulses and intuitions which were noticed in those interesting seasons of prayer could not have been all accidental nor could they be classed under the natural laws of cause and effect. The connection between the cause as seen in the prayer and the effect as related in the " happened-to-think " result is often wholly hidden.

A mother in Philadelphia prayed for her prodigal son and at that exact time the son, alone in a Chicago hotel, felt an uncontrollable influence to turn back to his home. A father prayed that his son might decide to be a missionary, and the son, a sailor off the coast of South America, at that same moment made the decision. A wife prayed that her husband might be sent home sober. At the time she was kneeling by the kitchen table he was waiting at the saloon to be served with brandy, but he "happened to think " that his mother had prayed for him on her deathbed and he could not take the liquor.

A doctor, sadly defeated in his fight for the life of his patient, went to his bedroom and prayed for light, and he "happened to think" that the patient might have swallowed some piece of metal. There was no report of the like symptoms in any case he could find in the medical books. But so deep was the impression that he secured a powerful magnet and drew forth the death-dealing needle. A merchant had an offer for his entire stock which seemed favorable, and, as he was in need, the offer seemed providential. But while the suggestion from the pulpit that each worshiper pray for success in his occupation was being adopted, he prayed for his business. At that hour his son in

Denver was also praying in church. When he there thought of his father he decided fully to go home and enter business with him. So completely did he decide that the next morning he telegraphed to his surprised and delighted father that he would come home if his father needed his assistance. The joy of having his son at home again overcame his determination to complete a favorable bargain, and he declined the offer promptly. Before the son reached Philadelphia a sudden change in the paper market doubled the sale value of the father's stock.

One writer for a daily newspaper was meditating on some object of prayer in the silence of the praying congregation when the idea of a textbook on journalism for college use came to his mind for the first time. It led directly to a series of syndicate articles which enabled him to purchase the home for which he had been praying. A mechanic who had been out of work, owing to a fire, prayed for a job. At the same time a builder who was a stranger in the church was praying for a competent partner. When the prayers were finished they "happened" to look at each other across the church and each wondered why the other looked at him so intently. The pews in which they sat were at right angles and it was a natural thing for the occupant of one pew to glance at the inmate of the other pew. After church each approached the other with the simultaneous expression, "It seems to me that we have met before." But that was their first meeting. Their firm is now engaged in large construction work in concrete houses and factories.

A servant girl in a small home prayed for a dress suitable for church and at that hour her mistress was visiting a friend who remarked that the photograph of a deceased daughter greatly resembled the visitor's servant girl. A few minutes later the friend of the mistress said: "I wonder if my daughter's dresses would fit your servant? If they will fit her, there are here two new gowns that the dressmaker sent home after my daughter's death."

So a young man, without advanced education, prayed hard for an opportunity to get mental training to fit him for the ministry. At the same moment a principal of a New Jersey academy was in the gallery far removed from the young man and he prayed for direction in finding a suitable janitor. The academy principal mentioned his need to one of the church members who "happened" to know the young man. It was arranged that the young man should work for his board and tuition and have five hours a day for study. The worshiper described himself in his sketch of the answer to his prayers as one whom "God has led into the fulfillment of all his highest ambitions." He is pastor of a strong church in Cleveland.

A little tot prayed for a "singing doll," and her mother told her that a doll was too small a matter to pray for. But the father overheard the conversation, and, after purchasing the most costly one he could find at his noon hour, he left it on the little one's bed in the night when everyone else was supposed to be asleep. A widow prayed for some leadership in the sale of some wild land in Louisiana. Her relatives urged her to let it go, as the "taxes will soon eat it all." But the unexpected payment of a debt due her led her to feel that, as she had been temporarily provided for, she would wait. In about seven weeks she read in a paper that a company had struck oil on the next section to her estate. She consequently leased the mineral privileges of her land at a high price.

A student whose mental faculties were unusually dull for his age prayed that he might pass his examination in mathematics. That night in his dreams his subconscious self worked out plainly on a blackboard the two hardest problems. A farmer prayed for some deciding hint in his choice of seed for his land. On his way home he held a bundle in his lap which was in a newspaper wrapper. In one column on the wrapper directly under his eyes was an article on the soils and products of his country which opened his vision and made his farming safe and profitable. An Alsatian girl prayed that her father and mother might come to America. They knew nothing of her petition, but on that same day and hour, allowing for the difference in the reckoning of time, the parents resolved to come to America, and financial aid was promised them.

A lawyer was asking the Lord for some clue to lost evidence, so necessary to his case to be tried the next day, when the name of a witness whose relation to the case he had not before thought of, and whose name had been long forgotten, was suggested to him. While doubtful of the value of the witness, he sought his name in the directory and found that the lost witness was all-sufficient for the case. A dealer in real estate asked the Lord to prosper a proposed transaction, if it were for the best, and to hinder it if it would be injurious. He unintentionally omitted the word "not" from the draft of a contract which he drew the next day and the "accidental" omission brought him to unexpected possession of a profitable block of houses.

To the unbeliever, all these testimonials prove but little. But to the experienced observer of repeated answers to prayer, they are conclusive proofs of God's disposition to answer the "effectual, fervent prayer of the righteous man." As a woman may feel when she puts her weary life into the care of a strong and affectionate husband, the trusting believer in prayer rests in God in a peaceful condition of soul which passeth all understanding.

Chapter VII - Day of Pentecost

THAT great day at the Baptist Temple stands out in the history of the local church. No one who entered personally, body and soul, into the services of that Easter in Philadelphia can possibly forget the overpowering impressions of the Divine Spirit. For the sake of a careful examination of the question whether the initiation of the spirit is of God or men, the plain facts are here stated.

It was Easter morning, 1893, when the sun began to gild the City Hall tower. People flocked to the lower hall of the Temple from all directions. Each greeted the other and faces glowed as they assembled. There was no prearranged program and no announcements. The people began to sing with enthusiasm before the leader ascended the platform. Then came the moment of silent prayer. It seemed as if "the place was shaken." The whole company trembled as if they realized they were in the visible presence of the Almighty. The most conservative shed tears.

There were many brief expressions from the audience, and often three were speaking at the same time. There was no shouting, no riotous disorder, no wild movements of uncontrolled emotion. Excited crowds at political gatherings, angry mobs, and panic-stricken crowds seem to have a form of that emotional common pressure. But that Easter gathering was a surrender of soul to the telepathic influence of a common spirit.

There was an intermission of an hour before the morning preaching service in the auditorium. But the people would not go out for breakfast. Some fasted all day. They talked about God and exchanged promises to pray for friends, for missions, and for churches. Before the hour of the established morning service the large upper Temple had overflowed. There had been no advertisement of the services. There were no unusual decorations of the auditorium and no special music provided. The preacher had not prepared a sermon, nor had he read over that morning a selected chapter. He had been too much crowded with visitors and pressing calls of the needy and dying to devote even a half an hour to mental preparation. But no feeling of doubt or of weakness entered his heart. He felt a strange support and uplift of soul which kept away all fears. He had not decided to preach at all, and hesitated whether he had not best venture on an "experience meeting " in the time usually allowed for the Easter sermon.

But the choir was inspired; they, too, felt the impression of a solemn convocation. They never sang like that before, and the old tunes were vibrant with a resurrection life. The people sang and wept. City officials, principals of the schools, court judges, and merchants, let the tears fall. There seemed to be an absolute surrender of all classes to a common pressure toward God. The preacher arose with a most powerful impulse to kneel and weep. He forgot to announce a text, but he began to talk brokenly from his heart.

To himself he seemed to be taken out of his physical limitations. He was not himself.
He was a higher personality. He saw visions of beauty and heard the harps of Glory. He lacked no words or thoughts. He spoke the ideas which were given him. There is no other joy on earth with which to compare that. It is so unlike the richest or sweetest emotions which other forms of happiness awaken. It is supreme! Unaccountable things occurred that morning which no prolonged or hard study has explained. The preacher cannot feel sure that he was inspired, and hesitates to mention the facts lest men should doubt their truth or ascribe to him an egotistical claim to sanctity. But the experience with that sermon, and sometimes with other addresses, presents a psychological study which none of the authorities on mental law have yet explained.

The stenographic report of the sermon showed that the speaker quoted from Homer, Justinian, Macaulay, Shakespeare, Longfellow, and Moliére accurately, without hesitation, in the onrush of his excited speech. But when he read them in the shorthand report he could not remember that he ever had read those quotations and was absolutely unable to recall that he used such words. He has tried to account for the quotations by accrediting them to the telepathic influence of stronger minds in the audience who were familiar with them. But that, too, can be only a guess. The mystery is not cleared up by such speculation. Perhaps the preacher should have called in someone else to write this chapter; but that "someone else" is not on call.

Hence, these incidents are set down without a claim to uncommon inspiration.
Probably thousands of priests and preachers have felt a like exaltation. But the closing hymn which began with general participation by all the people was so broken before its close that the last verse was carried only by a few. The people wept for joy. The preacher knelt at his chair and prayed for aid to lead in the prayer and benediction. But the benediction was not heard, and the audience was slowly convinced that the benediction had been pronounced by the observation that the minister dropped his hands and walked away.

The Bible-school service in the afternoon was as solemn and impressive as the morning.
Many of the hundreds baptized that day expressed themselves as having felt the dovelike Spirit of Peace descending on them, too. Nearly, if not all, the scholars and visitors turned sincerely and permanently to the Lord. The evening services were given up wholly to praise. The rejoicing was deep and strong. The crowd standing in the aisles and on the steps did not move until after the benediction. The number of those in the sittings was three thousand one hundred and thirty-four, and of those standing who got inside the doors was seven hundred and eighty-three. Over seven thousand converts have been taken into the membership of the Temple in thirty-nine years, but they have not been the direct results of seasons of special revival.

Great were the expectations of the church at that Easter as they prepared for a great immediate harvest. But it was not gathered then. The great Pentecostal visitation seemed to have had another purpose. The members of the church had in the Pentecost received a new instigation of spiritual fire, and the interest in missions and in the Bible was greatly increased. Five missions were established which soon became strong churches. Young men arose by the score to study for the ministry, and large gifts were made to the Temple University. Many kinds of local enterprises for the poor, the drunken, foreigners, and the aged were opened in the city and suburbs.

Chapter VIII - Axioms

THE prayerful soul must be sure that "God is," and the religious soul must believe in a real Divine Being. One condition necessary to successful prayer is a fixed belief in the Maker of all things. The religious person should keep his brain supplied with "axioms."

An axiom is a self-evident truth, an immovable, unchangeable fact. It is a fundamental principle of which all sane men are cognizant. It is a statement of truth which is below and above all argument - a truth which all men recognize as a part of their mental existence. An axiom is simply a reference to a necessary condition in the framework of the human constitution. Every living man acts on those conditions, whether he recognizes them or not. The man whose common sense recognizes those immovable principles builds his belief and action on them safely. Prayer, like all other religious things or conditions, needs to have a sure foundation. Therefore, axioms which are used as the basis of mathematical science are true everywhere, and the worshiper needs to recognize them as fully as the civil engineer.

Here are presented some of the axioms on which the believer safely rests his faith. They cannot be proven, because they are vitally and essentially true. Their nonexistence is positively unthinkable. If these axioms are not essential to all mental action, then the world is a dreamy unreality.

"Two parallel lines will never run together or cross each other." All recognize the absolute truth of the statement, and yet no one ever went to the end of the lines to get local evidence of the fact. "Two halves are equal to the whole," states the college professor before his class. He would be an idiot if he tried to "prove it." He may illustrate the idea by cutting an apple into halves and putting them together again. But the essential truth of the proposition every mind had accepted before he mentioned it.

"Two quantities or objects which are equal to a third quantity or object are equal to each other." A boy smiles at the waste of time in telling him such an axiomatic or self-evident fact. But the instructor is not attempting to inculcate a new principle, but rather to call attention emphatically to an immovable fact woven into the vital fabric of all human minds. The thinker who stands squarely on those fundamental facts can trust himself and can be trusted by all.

A careful review of one thousand and twenty letters relating to established cases of successful prayer showed that the believer accepted as fundamentally true axiomatic facts of which the following is a partial list. We know only because the mental knowledge is an essential part of our intellectual existence. We therefore know:

That two and two make four.
That we exist.
That we are independent, thinking beings.
That there is moral obligation to do right.
That there is good and evil.
That our essential self is not the body.
That every effect has an adequate cause.
That all things made had a Maker.
That there must have been a First Cause.
That all things change.
That nothing can be annihilated.
That wickedness should be punished.
That goodness should be rewarded.
That all happiness depends on the state of mind.
That there is a permeating spirit moving on all the events about mankind.
That man must eat to live.
That when man has done his best, yet his success still depends on Providence - often called Good Fortune or Good Luck.
That prayer can influence external conditions.
That light is not darkness.
That love is not hate.
That up is not down.
That the future is not the past.
That all men must leave the body.
That mankind is sinful.

That somewhere justice must be done to clear up the inequalities of this life.

That men essentially evil would not be at home or welcomed in a heaven occupied only by the good.

That worshiping an ideal of perfect righteousness makes the worshiper like the ideal, as a perfect model makes a more perfect statue.

That some things have more intrinsic value than others.

That the highest satisfaction of soul is in the communion with God.

That the soul is indestructible and must live forever.

These axioms are unchangeably true, and all doubts or attempts to "prove" them bring only confusion and partial insanity. To doubt generally that we see or feel or smell or think is to undermine all knowledge and to make life a crazy jumble. Some things we do know; it is suicidal to doubt them. These are mankind's chief good. They constitute the world's greatest treasure, which is "everyday common sense." If common sense, unadulterated, be given, any man he will worship God. The keenest scientist cannot safely leap off that one ship.

One of the testimonials wherein the author, who was never a student in the "school of doubt," tells why he came to feel the necessity of prayer relates to one day's experience. He had decided, after much thought, just how he would use his time before he left his little home in the morning. He had made up his mind to take a trolley car, but a heavy truck had fallen on the track, so he was compelled to change his plan and walk. He reached his small store one half hour late, and a customer that he had arranged to meet had called and gone. He intended to call on a salesman, of whom he was to purchase a new stock of goods, and the telephone was out of order, owing to the effects of the electricity of a distant thunderstorm. He sent for a cab for the purpose of visiting the salesman at the hotel in another part of the city, but the horse attached to the cab fell at the store door and broke necessary parts of the harness. The accident made his proposed trip useless, because of the delay. He ordered his lunch which he usually ate in the back store, but he did not get time to eat it, owing to a visit from a salesman from New York, who wished him to take a large bankrupt stock of a new line of goods. The coming profits seemed large and sure. He would have missed that trade had the car been on time or the telephone in order or had the horse not fallen. Even the lunch he had so confidently expected to eat was thrown away.

He went home at night with an entire change in his plans, and entered on a new line of trade. His wife was absent, attending on a sick neighbor, and his evening paper was too torn to read. When he knelt at his bedside that night to pray, the feeling of utter dependence on God's providence made him throw himself on the Lord as he had never done before. And after he was in bed he could hear his daughter entertaining her company in the parlor by singing, "I'll go where He wants me to go." That merchant was a man of great discernment and honest daily piety, and is said to have acted as agent for the government in the wartime in the purchase of ninety millions' worth of his line of goods.

Another writer told of a young student for the ministry who came home on a visit to his village church and tried to prove that the world was not created by a personal God, that "evil and sickness are only delusions," and that "we do not exist". But an old farmer, noted for honesty, and whose common sense had caused the people to insist on his holding for years the office of mayor, arose after that leader of the meeting sat down, and remarked, "I still believe that, after all that has been said, my cows are real cows, and my wife is real, God is real, and my tax bills are real; and I believe that that young man will some day come to himself, and admit that he was a theological idiot." But that old farmer also testified that he did not feel the need of asking God for definite things, but declared that prayer was his daily recreation, and all things worked together for good.

Chapter IX - Praying for Money

IN all the forty years of praying, of which only a partial record could be kept, there was no topic more satisfactory than the experience of such a large company in praying for money. There was no prearranged plan of procedure and no speculative purpose to obtain the help of God in the accumulation of property. But for some reason, which is not now recalled, there was given out for an evening's meditation the topic, "Shall we pray for money?" There was a strong division of opinion, some asserting that we are not authorized to pray for anything but for the Holy Spirit. Others asserted with complete confidence that prayer should be made for anything which we felt we needed. The majority appeared to be assured that men must work and seek only "the kingdom of God," and that they should believe that all other things would be given from God as we should have need.

Fortunately or providentially the men and women who held to the theory that God commands his disciples to pray for money determined to put the matter to a fair test. They were led by a consecrated deacon at whose house they held the weekly meetings.
They did not ask the Lord for money at first, but prayed daily for instruction on the important question whether it was a duty, or was permissible, for men to pray for success in their secular business. There were four men and several businesswomen whose experience was especially valuable. One of them was the owner or partner in a bookbindery. The company of believers devoted an entire evening to prayer for the prosperity of his business. They agreed, further, to pray for that one thing in unison at twelve o'clock each day for one week. The conditions were especially for observation, as the owner of the business was a devout, unselfish soul who had determined, years before, to give a tenth of all his income to the Lord's work, and he stood willing to give his all if any good cause demanded such a sacrifice.

The first week was without visible result, and some who were weak in faith abandoned the attempt to test the matter in that way. But the small number left began to study favorable answer. Their first conclusion was that it is right to ask the Lord for the necessities of life, which always included food, clothing, shelter, health, and worship.

The good deacon stated that he had all of those things. He, however, stated that he owed quite a large sum in his business obligations, and he had prayed to the Lord to aid him in paying his debts. Then with one accord that company decided to pray for that one thing.

The amount of the debts cannot now be recalled, but it was several thousand dollars, contracted for business furniture and machinery. Although there are several witnesses living, it is difficult to state with assured accuracy the amounts involved. But to those who shared in the experiment the principal facts stand out clearly in the memory. The first noon prayer was on Wednesday, which was the day following the prayer meeting. The deacon, after his noon lunch, went into a publishing house on Chestnut Street, as was his custom almost daily. There he was introduced to a gentleman from Washington, D. C., who told the deacon that "for the first time in life" he had forgotten his train. He did not know the deacon's business when he told the deacon that he must return to Washington without visiting New York, as his business in Washington could not be left longer without immediate attention. But in his explanation he mentioned that he intended to give out a contract in New York for the binding of blank books for the government. When the deacon mentioned the fact that he was a bookbinder, and doing the same kind of work, immediately the gentleman became interested, and remarked that he did not know before that such work could be done in Philadelphia. He made some inquiry in the store and, finding the deacon's reputation for integrity and honesty was very high, he arranged with the deacon to put in new machinery, to hire another floor in the building, and agreed that the government should make an advance payment on the first order.

The deacon hurried to another member of the prayer circle who was a jeweler also on Chestnut Street and, with a tear, declared that the Lord had already shown his hand in his business. The third day, as the deacon was looking at some machinery, the salesman told the deacon that he had heard that a New York bindery was going out of business on account of a larger opportunity for the firm in another line of work, and the salesman advised the deacon to go over and see it. When the next weekly meeting of the prayer circle was held the deacon had bought in New York all the machinery that he needed, all in good condition, and at an astonishingly low price.

Ever after that, the deacon, when he entered his office in the morning, shut himself in for ten minutes and prayed for the Lord's direction in his business. Another prayer test followed by the agreement of that prayer circle to pray for the jeweler, who was one of the circle and whose business was in a most deplorable condition. The jeweler was old and forgetful, and his son had moved out of the city rather than stay among his acquaintances when the inevitable financial wreck should come. The jeweler stated his condition fully to the meeting, and even declared his intention of calling a meeting of his creditors as a preliminary to bankruptcy proceedings. He said that the condition was so manifestly his own fault that all he dared ask of the Lord was that the creditors would be lenient toward him.

Two or three days after that meeting the jeweler's son was called to Philadelphia to attend the funeral of a member of his wife's family. After the funeral, while talking with a manufacturer from Baltimore, who was one of the mourners, the son said that his father was a first-class clock maker of forty years' experience, but that he was unfitted for the management of finances. The manufacturer said that he needed an experienced man to superintend a new factory in Baltimore, then under construction. The son advised his father to write to the manufacturer for the job to begin work when he should close his Chestnut Street store. The jeweler wrote a long description of his troubles, and asked for employment. The manufacturer, after receiving it, took a train to Philadelphia and then spent the afternoon and the greater part of the night in trying to make a reasonable estimation of the value of the Chestnut Street business. The outcome of that examination was that the manufacturer took over the whole business, paid off the debts, and formed partnership with the jeweler which opened into a prosperous trade.

An old lady who must have been one of that prayer circle wrote that she recalled the
fact that the circle agreed to pray for her business, which was then a "notion store" on Columbia Avenue, Philadelphia. She writes that soon after the united prayer for her business began there was a fire which destroyed the store next to her lot. In the reconstruction of the next store the owner was anxious to build larger and offered her an unexpectedly large sum as a bonus and also desired to combine in a partnership with her to put both stores into one general store. The bonus she invested in an annuity, and the business afterward paid her enough to live in all the comforts of a cultured life.

It is said that everyone of that prayer circle became prosperous, but it may be helpful to mention one more of the most remarkable cases. A young clerk in a great national bank, who came from a farm learn what he could there of finances, stated freely that he was getting all that he was worth to the bank, and that he was contented with his financial condition. He told the circle that he did not wish to be included in their prayer list. But when the reports began to come in of the successful prayers and the circle grew in numbers and in interest, he began to consider how much more good he could do if he had a larger income. He handled thousands of dollars daily, and checked up often the accounts of prosperous and generous businessmen of the city. At last, the desire to be of more use to the Lord led him to begin to pray for money. Finally, he confessed his changed attitude and asked the circle to give one week of prayer for him.

A few days later an epidemic of the grippe laid in bed all but three of the bank's employees. One day the assistant cashier and the clerk were the only persons on time at the opening of the bank. They persuaded a vice president of another bank to come to their assistance, and he was so impressed with the young clerk's efficiency and coolness that he offered him the place of assistant cashier in his own bank. The position was finally accepted, and led to his promotion, a few years after, to the presidency of the bank.

The experience of that prayer circle was more or less the general experience of the church members. The suggestions of a church service, the aid to an honest and industrious life, and the greater health of church members, generally confirm everywhere the fact that faith and habits are surely the most favorable for "the life that now is, as well as for the life which is to come."

In connection with this phase of our narrative there should be written a brief account of an experience which surprised even the most conservative minds. Appeals for subscriptions have been made rarely in the Temple. Such appeals have accomplished but little. The regular gifts of the many persons have steadily paid all expenses and provided enough over to finally pay off all debts. But there were seasons when unusual sums were needed and when the money was furnished from some unexpected sources seemingly in direct answers to special prayer. On one occasion there was an especially large sum given into the treasury when it was imperatively needed and when no notice of the need had been given from the pulpit. On one Sunday morning the preacher could find no other satisfactory subject on which to build a sermon, and he talked with the people about the Bible school lesson for that day. The subject included a description of how the Jews were required to select the best lamb of the flock for an offering to God. They did not hope that God would hear their prayers unless they gave their best to the Lord. The sermon closed with a sentence or two of application to our own times. The emphatic exhortation stated that offerings and prayers should go together, but the offering should precede the prayer.

At the evening service some person sent to the pulpit a note, asking that the printed order of services "be changed so as, thereafter, to substitute the word 'offering' for the word 'collection.' " The minister, acting on the impulse of the moment, announced a change in the order of the services, and said that as the ancient custom of making an offering before asking the Lord for a gift or blessing was surely acceptable to God, an "offering" would be taken before the prayer, instead of after the prayer. No unusual sum came in that evening. The notes of the church were coming due ten days later, but those debts were not thought of by minister or ushers in any relation to that offering, though prayers were often made for the help of the Lord in the payment of the debt.

The following Sunday morning the collection was said to be the largest ever received by the ushers; while the fact was not mentioned from the pulpit, it was the subject of general comment among the people after service. At the evening service the offering was so great that one of the ushers related how he had to go out and empty the basket he was passing and come back to finish taking the offering: Nothing else had been done or said, and the church notes were paid as a matter of course. But the prayers made that day were made immediately before the offering was taken. The question was put to the audience twice to ascertain if anyone who made a special offering on that particular day had not been answered, and there was no exception in the mass of testimony to the efficiency of each prayer that day.

The recitals of the marvels which followed that prayerful offering were too startling for general belief. The reports may have been exaggerated in the time of such general excitement, but the people had complied with the conditions, and God had answered clearly according to his promise. They had "brought the tithes into the storehouse," and the Lord had poured out the blessings as an infallible result. The letters which came to the officials of the church relating incidents concerning the effects of the prayers made that day were not filed then as they have been in later years, and the record here must depend wholly on the memory of two or three witnesses.

The following partial list of cases is very nearly correct. The cases of sudden and in some cases instantaneous recovery of the sick were related by hundreds of people. In one case a poor man whose only living child was insane put his money into the basket that morning and prayed for his child's recovery. Both he and she often declared that while being forcibly given a cold bath at the time that offering was made she felt "a loud report in her head like the report of a pistol," and her mind was found to be normal in all respects from that instant. The father went to the sanitarium that afternoon, as was his custom on the

Sabbath, and his daughter met him at the door in her right mind.

A lady sold her best clothes and all her jewelry on Saturday and brought the whole of the proceeds and gave all as an offering as she prayed for her own healing. She suffered greatly from sciatic rheumatism, inherited from several generations. She fell on the front steps of the church, as they were helping her to the carriage, and arose to find the pain had permanently disappeared.

One old gentleman who was involved in a ruinous lawsuit over a lease of his little shop brought all the profits of the previous week and deposited them as he prayed for a legal and just victory. The next day or on the second day, his goods were so badly damaged by the smoke and water caused by a fire in the store next door, that the insurance company took the stock at his valuation and the landlord withdrew his suit.

Another case generally believed, but not fully confirmed, was of an Englishman who, not having money enough to pay his fare to Australia, deposited all that he did have into the offering and prayed for his passage. It was asserted and not contradicted that he found a one-hundred-dollar bill the next day in his wallet or in his bureau drawer, placed there by some friend whom he could not discover. Another related how she determined to risk all on one prayer, and gave all as she prayed. When the plumbers came to repair a leak the next week after the prayer, they discovered a loose board in the floor under which her father had secretly hidden his money. The sum she found was much more than enough to pay off the overdue mortgage on her cottage.

There were probably fifty such cases reported in detail at the time. But a solemn sense of sacredness connected with those experiences pervaded the assemblies, and no notice of the cases was given from the pulpit. And yet a calm and careful examination of the results of that exercise of faith has often suggested a strong doubt whether that experience did not do more harm than good.

The direct and immediate results convinced the devout believers that when a true servant of God makes a sincere offering, God will invariably accept the offering and answer in some manner his petition fully. But it seems impossible to find the line between the motives which may make an offering acceptable or unacceptable to God. The remarkable success of that day of offering led many to believe that they could drive a bargain with the Lord. Absurd as it seems, there were many earnest people who believed that they could invest a small sum in an offering and by asking for a large sum would make an immense profit in the transaction. A dangerous spirit of gambling arose. Noble men and women were caught in a theological net spread by the spirit of evil. The heavens soon became brass and no offering seemed acceptable. It was a dangerous period in the history of the church. Some gave up all faith in prayer. The speculative spirit led some to give largely with a hope of a hundredfold return. The treasury of the church was being filled rapidly, but there were divisions over the investment of the money. Some strong members left the church, while several counted their offerings as a dead loss and went back "into the world " altogether.

But there is left a good foundation for a consistent belief in the power of consistent prayer in producing objective results. While it may be difficult for a human father to discern between the motives of his child who brings him a gift so as to be sure that the gift is the exhibition of a pure affection, yet the Lord has no such limitation. He knows whether the offering is a gambling venture or a lovely deed inspired by a pure, unselfish love. God does love and does answer a cheerful giver. The loving son remembers the unselfish devotion of his mother and the offerings she gave him without thought of any return or reward and his delight to have her ask him to do for her. God is love, and he loves the lover. His intrinsic nature compels him to answer the call of his beloved. But he cannot be driven or tricked into granting the prayer of a greedy deceiver whose whole motive is selfish. The idea is foolishly unrighteous which looks upon the arrangement of Providence as a slot machine into which the pretended worshiper may put a copper penny and draw out a gold dollar. As gold must be given for gold, so love must be given for love.

Chapter X - Unanswered Prayers

THE many letters which report that prayers have not been answered made the examination into that department of the investigation to be most discouraging until the testimonies were read the second or third time. Slowly it dawned on the reader that the ~ writers did not know, after all, whether their prayers were answered or not. A bright light was let in on the subject by the expression of one who stated that he had prayed for the meals to pay off a mortgage on his home until he had abandoned all hope and had decided to sell his house to the railroad company for a siding. In answer to a later inquiry the discouraged petitioner stated that the jury, to which by contract both parties agreed to leave the assessment of the "land damages," had given him money enough to buy a much finer home away from the continual annoyance of passing trains.

Many of the wholly disappointed petitioners closed their complaints or doleful faultfinding outbursts with the stereotyped quotation, "nevertheless, not my will, but Thine be done !" To some "the heavens are as brass"; to others, their prayers did not go "higher than their heads," and to still others their prayers became meaningless and like "words called into the thin air." This phase of our topic could not be followed up as far as a careful investigator could wish, because it involved so much correspondence and so much delay. But a general statement of the conclusions reached by those whose prayers had, seemingly, not been answered can be safely made. They all naturally and necessarily formed a concept of God by imagining him to be an all-mighty and all-good man. The human mind seems incapable of forming any other idea of God than can be obtained from a human model, greatly enlarged.

Human kings, human fathers, human saints, human sinners are really pictured in the minds of all who strive to visualize the Almighty or the angels. No Hindu can even think Nirvana. No mind can meditate on nothing. Everything conceived in the mind must be like something else. Reasoning from "the known to the unknown," or "the lesser to the greater," is the only possible process by which man can know God. So all those seemingly defeated ones had looked up to God as to a great man, and when he seemed to do nothing in answer to their requests they concluded that he either did not hear or that he would not even reply.

They did not think, however, of their heavenly Father as they would of an earthly father who was perfectly good. A good and wise father must often deny his child the article for which he asks, but he will not dismiss the matter with a curt denial. He will try to find something else for his child, as has been already stated in a previous chapter. The testimonies which asserted that the all-good God had denied or ignored the requests of his followers were the strongest proofs of the fact that God had granted their requests. The father who would not give a stone to his child who asked for bread would not give a stone to his starving child who asked for a stone. In those seasons when the attention of the people was centered specially on the results of prayer there was often heard the expression, "Perhaps He sees that it is best for me that I should not get the blessing for which I asked." But a consensus of opinion taken from the mass of correspondence showed a general belief that there are no unanswered prayers. They believed that in some other way which was better and wiser God sent his child a more valuable token
of his love.

Those reports gave the student an insight into the popular religious beliefs of the common people. The theological creeds and formulas which are found in the libraries are written by talented, studious scholars who put their own conclusion into print and do not attempt to set out the opinions retained by the masses. Often a silent congregation retains a strong belief in some theological idea which the preacher does not recognize. Often the minister of a church, having the reputation of being firmly orthodox, teaches theories which are not accepted by his hearers. Hence, the scrutiny of all that correspondence covering so many years gave an insight into the faith of the everyday Christian which was enlightening and helpful.

The testimony came from a much wider circle than the actual membership of that church, as visitors at the Temple from other quarters of the earth sent in their accounts of the way the Lord had answered their prayers. In those letters some remark or some statement often unconsciously disclosed this belief relating to prayer. Their beliefs concerning death, the Judgment, the future life, the methods used by the Lord in his administration, and the occupations of the saints in heaven most strangely harmonized when a careful digest was made.

The divine plan of salvation and the Creator's purpose revealed in natural law were sometimes quite at variance with the dogmas of the pulpit. But the common theories came out so distinctly that a statement of them is a matter of no difficulty. The common people connected directly or indirectly with the Christian churches believe:

That every person lives on as an individual after the body dies.
That the life on earth determines the state of happiness or misery in the spiritual existence.
That the soul is of the same substance as that of the angels.
That the occupation of the redeemed in the spirit world is the same as that of the angels.
That the departed persons know one another and keep company with those they have loved and known on earth.
That they serve God as his messengers to the inhabitants of the earth.
That they cannot be called nor can they visit the earth unless especially sent by the Almighty.
That the condition of the wicked or of those unfit for God's service in heaven is unknown.
That after the Judgment there may come the annihilation of the wicked.
That heaven is a condition of everlasting progress in knowledge.
That salvation depends on the intrinsic character, and that a conversion is a conversion to a godly character.
That many of the ceremonies of the churches are useless, and that the various denominations should endeavor to unite in some one federation.
That God is gradually building up a perfect human race on earth.
That he commands his servants to come to his aid in securing that end.
That the best or only way to fit ourselves for heaven is in the practice and discipline of helping humanity in the development of a higher race.

But the consensus of the opinion which related to prayer and the methods the Lord adopts to convey his answers should have special notice here. There was a decided agreement in their imaginative conception of the way the Lord arranged for the conveyance of his decisions to those who call upon him.

They hold in common that God is "immanent" in nature, and his replies to our requests may come as quietly and mysteriously as God's answer to the farmer who, in an act which is a prayer, places a seed in the ground.

Many testified to their belief that "all things work together" in producing the effects of prayer on those who love God. Nearly all, also, believed that God often called an angel to him when the prayer of faith came to him from the earth, and that he gave the angel personal instructions to visit the petitioner and aid him or her. The views of the Bible and its doctrines, according to the general opinion, appear to be that it is the best book ever written, and that it was inspired by a purpose so pure and unselfish as to be divine. One old lady expressed the general sentiment of the entire body when she wrote that, "the Bible is the best book I know of, and it is the only one which tells me about heaven, and I don't let any fool of a scholar argue it out of my life."

The number of readers of the Bible is much larger than the estimate which many modern writers give. The Sabbath school and haphazard pulpit essays have not so completely supplanted the home study of the Scriptures, as has been so often stated. The use of the Bible as the standard of moral character continues to be the practice of millions who may not study it closely or may not read it at all. That miracle-working Book is still a most powerful moral force in all departments of our civilized life. No patriot or respectable scholar can ignore the value of the Bible as the highest literature or as the foundation for all just human laws.

The people do believe in it.

Chapter XI - Prayer for Others

ALTHOUGH it is difficult to divide the subject of prayer into clearly separate departments, yet, for the purpose of concentrating the thought of the reader, and with the idea of emphasizing the importance of the events selected, this chapter has been set apart for special discussion. The possible relation of the law of mental telepathy to this experience has already been suggested and need not be repeated here. But the recent general sympathy with the parents of a child which was stolen led many people to pray for the recovery of the precious little one.

At the Temple in 1889 such a case was presented at the church services and an appeal made to the people to ask the Lord to influence the kidnapers to bring back the child. That led to the discussion of many previous cases where the parents believed that their lost child was returned to them in answer to prayer. In two cases each child was carefully deposited at the door of its parents. In both cases they had held special meetings of their neighbors to pray for the return of their child, and in one case they had appealed to the priest for his intercession. If the Lord used his direct power to bring the child home it must have been used through some event or some direct suggestion having an influence on the minds of the captors, because in the cases here mentioned there was no clue revealed which could lead to the abductors.

.

But an older case may illustrate what most probably did occur in other instances.

In 1889 a child two years of age was stolen from the front yard of a home in Charlestown, Massachusetts (now a part of Boston). A large ransom was demanded which was far beyond the reach of the parents. After several weeks of excited search by all the police organizations of the nation, the child was secretly returned, without ransom, and left cheerfully rapping on its parents' door. One of the robber gang who had conspired to steal children for ransoms, and who had laid the successful plan to capture that child, was arrested several days after the return of the child and confessed his share in the crime. His account of the influences and events which led to the restoration of the child was a most impressive and convincing illustration of the spiritual forces God may use in such cases.

The band of four robbers could not quiet the child when they carried him away, and they resorted to a gag which nearly killed the child. But the frightened little fellow screamed whenever the gag was taken from his mouth and would not eat or drink.
The child was evidently near to death. Then one of the robbers carried the child to a woman who occupied a room over a saloon in Brooklyn, New York. The woman was able to pacify the child, and explained to acquaintances that the child was an orphan whose mother, a near relation, had just died. The woman knew that the child was being held for a ransom, of which she was promised a large share. But she did not know from what part of the country the child came. She was an irreligious, coarse, profane woman, and cared only for money and drink. But one day she sent a letter to the resort of the gang and told them that she had a clear presentiment that something dreadful would happen to them if they did not hurry up the business of returning the child. As they paid no attention to her warnings she wrote again, saying that she would keep the child but ten days longer. They then visited her or wrote to her to care for the child three weeks longer, as they were sure of the "swag" by that time.

In the following week one of the gang was caught by the foot in a falling window sash as he tried to leap to a fire escape and he was burned to death while he hung there. The hotel was in full blaze when he awoke and his only possible escape was by that window. Another one of the gang swallowed a broken glass button when hastily eating a piece of biscuit at a railroad restaurant. . He was taken to a hospital or sanitarium in Montreal, where after long agony he died, and his body was buried in the public ground.

When the woman who held the child heard of that she took the child boldly to the house where the other three or four abductors met and flatly told them that all of them would come under a curse if they did not return that child to his parents. But they made a joke of their comrades' death, and gave her brandy until she wandered home

72

drunk. The child was then placed in charge of a poor widow in Hoboken, who was told that the mother was dead and the father was at sea, but would soon return. They paid liberally in advance for the child's board, and none of the circumstances awakened the least suspicion in the widow's mind. One night she slept with the child's arm across her neck. She awoke with a dreadful feeling of being choked to death by a strong man who exclaimed, "That child is stolen, and you must appear before God at once to give an account." The details of her experiences are here quoted from the *New York Herald*:

The widow called it "a waking dream." She was so shocked by the experience that she would not keep the child and sent for the man who had brought the child and demanded that the child be at once taken away. She did not believe that her warning was a premonition of any crime nor that the child had been stolen, but she was in a state of strange terror and told the man who came for the child that she was too nervous to board so young a child.

It appears that when the robber returned to the usual rendezvous, after leaving the child at
an orphan asylum and agreeing to pay for the board of "his child," he found another member of the party down with a sudden and dangerous fever. Then he, too, was struck with an impression of coming doom. It remained upon him night and day. He became so intoxicated that he was locked in the jail. In the depression of his recovery from the drink he determined to kill himself. Then the idea that he might escape from his horror by taking the child back to its home became so insistent that as soon as he was released he went after the child and took it back on the night train. He told the lisping child to rap on his father's door and "call for papa." Then he hastened away and did not return to his former gang.

This authentic incident may or may not prove that prayer was answered, as it is not known what prayers were offered for that child's recovery. But it does show how the Lord may work in other cases where prayers are openly made. The angels of God are sent to pronounce curses on the disobedient sometimes, and terrible plagues are sent on men by them. Hence, the Lord does use various curses to work out his will and it seems reasonable to believe that he does warn men and women by terrible mental impressions.

This theory is strongly confirmed by the testimonies found in this large correspondence. Lost children were restored after prayers were made for them in startlingly impressive manners. At Cape May a fisherman obeyed a wholly unexplainable impulse and put back to the marshes, feeling that he had "left something." but unable to remember what it was. There he heard the cry of the lost child, wading waist deep in the incoming tide. A merchant of Wilmington, Delaware, wrote that his child was taken by the grandparents when his wife died, and after the grandparents died the child was hidden by the relatives. The reason for the action was because of a difference of religious faith. He began one day a regular system of prayer for the recovery of his child. He went to a fishing camp in the woods of Maine in August and his child came into his log hut for a drink of water. She was with a party who camped nearby in tents. Another stolen child was the little son of a doctor who prayed long and hard for the return of his little son. The sudden attack of chills felt by a passenger on a Hudson River boat at the pier caused the officers to call him on board from the wharf. The afflicted matron and his own child were in the same stateroom together.

One trustworthy officer of the church testified that his child had wandered away from the railroad station while he was asleep on the bench, and that he could not find her after an all-night search. He prayed at his family prayers, asking the Lord in sobs to protect and return his child. He said that an impression as strong as a voice insisted in his mind that he ought to search in some freight yards across the river. The yards were one mile from the station. He told his friends how he felt and insisted that he would go to the yards and search. There he found his starving child under an old fallen fence. He never could discover any satisfactory solution of the mystery of her presence in the railroad yards. She must have toddled the whole mile among vehicles in the night. He has firmly believed in guardian angels ever since that day.

There were numerous cases told of mental impressions made upon children away from home by the influence of a mother's prayer. To all of these incidents the skeptic will assert that, though there be millions of cases where men and women "happened to think" of the person praying at the moment the prayer was offered, it would not be conclusive proof that the thought was suggested by the prayer or in answer to it. But this suggestion presents other cases wherein it is far more difficult to disbelieve than it is to believe. The weight of evidence is almost overwhelmingly on the side of the religious believer.

The belief that God will so adjust his providences as to bring to a person friends, weather, business, health, and domestic peace in answer to the prayer of some insistent friend is almost universal. General Garibaldi stated that he found that his belief in the efficacy of his mother's prayers in securing protection of his life when in danger was accepted by all his friends as a statement which at least might be realized. The common-sense view is that where a theory cannot be subjected to proof either way it surely is wisest to believe in that view which has the strongest influence for good on the life and usefulness of the believer.

What a man believeth, as well as what he thinketh, determines what he is. He who believes in the efficacy of his father's or mother's prayers lives a nobler life than the skeptic. The friend who sincerely prays for you is a friend who would sacrifice most for you in case of need. Two lovers, separated far and praying long for each other, is an exhibition of the truest, sweetest love. It is, also, the best test of God's disposition to heed the requests of his children. No prayer for another can be felt to be effective which is not inspired more or less by real love. The loving heart is a large part of a great previous character. He or she has an intercessory disposition - an intrinsic tendency toward doing good, and that, with a strong, clean mind, makes a true God-like person. Such men are grateful to those who pray for them, and are impelled to pray for others. These are some of the reasons given why people ought always to pray.

Chapter XII - Forms of Prayer

IT appears that the extremest ritualist does not feel wholly bound to his prayer book. The people exercise great liberty in the choice of words or postures when they go to God in anxious prayer. Appropriate forms are reasonably sought for varying occasions, and some of the forms of prayer which are venerable for age and sublimity are reverenced and adopted because so often they best express the heart's sincere desire. The Lord's Prayer is recited with profit in a formal church service, but is seldom recited in time of extreme need. During the earthquake at San Francisco no one was known to have repeated the Lord's Prayer.

The exact words in English are not adjustable to every occasion. Men in earnest ask for what they need in their own words and in their own way. The effectual and fervent prayer of the righteous man availeth much because it is fervent and righteous. To be in every way right, and then to add the inspiration or fire or fervency, are conditions which only the righteous can fill. But, happily, the sinner is not required to be right in all things before his prayer is heard.

The stately dignity and beautiful phraseology of the Catholic churches, the impressive forms of the old English ritual, or the simple appeal of the mission worker are all alike acceptable to God when they are the expression of real heart worship or of a call for relief in some actual need. In the worship at the Baptist Temple there has been no form of prayer in which the people so sincerely and so generally joined as in the prayers found in some of the hymns. A study of the human or apparent agencies which may have had some influence does not fully account for the spirit of prayer which some hymns awaken.

A cool and analytical examination of this subject was made by the preacher one Sabbath morning for the purpose of recording it here. A relation of the plain facts, without using the circumstances to establish any sectarian theory, will most clearly set out the case before the impartial critic. The hymn chosen that morning for the opening of the service was selected chiefly because it is a prayer. The three verses are as follows:

Father, whate'er of earthly bliss
Thy sovereign will denies,
Accepted at thy throne of grace,
Let this petition rise:
Give me a calm, a thankful heart,
From every murmur free;
The blessings of thy grace impart,
And make me live to thee.
Let the sweet hope that thou art mine
My life and death attend,
Thy presence through my journey shine,
And crown my journey's end.

The people were everywhere in motion. Some were coming in, some were standing near the doors, some were talking in low voices in the rear of the deep gallery, and many were arranging for their wraps or hats, while all, in the freedom of the social atmosphere ever prevailing there, were smilingly nodding to acquaintances or searching for hymn books. The opening chorus of the Children's Church, at their regular service, in the lower hall, could be indistinctly heard. The painful and awkward silence which embarrasses and chills the incoming worshiper in some churches was altogether absent that morning. The preacher began to read the hymn without waiting for silence or attention. He simply remarked, "Let us sincerely and intelligently use this old hymn for our opening prayer." The congregation arose while the organist played a sweet, tender prelude, giving the impression that the organ itself was praying. A fair-haired child, kneeling in a snow-white night robe, lisping its evening prayer, was suggested to hundreds by the worshipful music. The well-trained religious chorus began to sing with devotion and unity and opened the prayer with the harmonious call, "Father ! " The congregation instinctively raised their eyes toward heaven. Then all came strongly into the hymn with the petition:

"Father, whate'er of earthly bliss
Thy sovereign will denies,
Accepted at thy throne of grace,
Let this petition rise:
"Give me a calm, a thankful heart,
From every murmur free;
The blessings of thy grace impart,
And make me live to thee."

There was a single strain of an interlude and then the solemn prayer was entered upon with an unction and appreciation that thrilled every soul in the great audience:

"Let the sweet hope that thou art mine
My life and death attend,
Thy presence through my journey shine,
And crown my journey's end."

Then came a pause, and with a magnificent volume of sound the emphatic "Amen!" confirmed the earnestness of the prayer.

That was a real prayer! The holiness of the spirit of worship had taken possession of the whole congregation. All were interested in the reading of the Bible, and when the notices were being read a most saintly old deacon sent up a slip of paper to the preacher on which were written these words -"Pastor, please give us another prayer for the next hymn!" The pastor read the note to the people without comment, and looked over the hymn book for another prayer.

When the hymn was announced and read deliberately the preacher said, feelingly, " Let us pray! " The prayer in that hymn was used by all. As they sang, their faces flushed. Old men shed tears, and the preacher decided, before the last verse was sung, to take for his theme the last two lines:

Hope shall change to glad fruition,

Faith to sight and *prayer* to *praise.*

The deep, soul-filled joy of the morning worship carried good cheer, hope, and courage into a thousand homes and made the week's labors enjoyable and prosperous.

In choosing the form of prayer the temperament and state of health of the worshiper may be an important consideration. But whether in hymns or psalms or gestures, the call must be earnestly sincere. When the formal, monotonous recitations of the customary church rituals are recalled it becomes a marvel that the church survives the pious hypocrisy and sacrilegious indifference of the church pulpits and altars. The pulpit is seen by all and the words and tones of the preacher are heard by all; the place is the most conspicuous in the church life; and if the action or the ceremony is hypocritical or careless there, then the whole church is permeated by the same spirit.

The form of expression must be a secondary consideration in all prayer, while appropriateness and custom have rightfully an influence on the petition. Yet the essential thing is in the natural cry of a needy soul. Prayer, as a public function, should be a stimulant or an instructor leading the individuals in the congregation to pray by and for themselves. The people must pray. The need of this was apparent in many of the requests made for prayer at the Temple in Philadelphia. "Lord, teach us to pray," is ever the appeal of the religious masses.

The union of two or three in concerted prayer for a definite thing was very effective. The observation of the same hour by many people has often developed a deep religious life and secured practical results. The testimony of one active businessman exhibited triumphantly the use of continuous prayer and may serve as a comprehensive illustration.

He wrote:
I fought it out with myself, knowing the Lord would work with me. When I awoke in the morning I thanked God for shelter and sleep. Then I began to pray for the least things of my morning preparations - my clothes, my bath,

my comb and brush, my articles used in any way. I thanked God for, and prayed for, the continuance of his kindness. I managed to keep in a state of prayer at the breakfast table. I prayed for instruction in purchasing the necessities of the home. I prayed as I left my door. I prayed along the street for wisdom to transact business. I prayed for the persons I met on my way. I prayed for the clerks, for the customers, for thoughts, for words, for farsightedness, for a contented disposition consistent with activity. If I wrote a letter I asked the Lord to aid me in the writing and to protect the letter on to its delivery. I did not speak aloud or tell people I was praying. I kept the Lord constantly in mind. I had some discouraging experiences with myself, but I kept pursuing the idea. At last it grew easy and enjoyable. It was in every way a success. I did not waste my money. I did not carelessly destroy articles I used. I did not overeat. I did not get angry with my employees. I felt a real interest in the welfare of others. I did my best and left all to God. It is now a settled habit. My health is almost perfect. Before I began to pray I was asthmatic and gouty. If this has anything boastful about it, the Lord forgive me. But in the request for my experience you insisted on "frankness in all accounts."

Whether it be possible for all to reach that prayerful condition and retain it permanently cannot be denied or asserted infallibly. But it is evident that but few reach it. The exhortation that is appropriate here appears to be to urge an honest effort to get as near to that devotional condition as possible and to hold all the ground we do gain.

Chapter XIII - Does God Answer Christians Only?

WHAT might be the consensus of opinion found in a digest of all the testimonies of mankind cannot be surmised, but it did not appear that God was a "respecter of persons " through those years of prayer at the Baptist Temple. The prevailing belief, however, was that God was more willing to answer the sincere disciple than he was to heed the requests of a great sinner. But the fact was also evident that God does answer the just and the unjust. The assertion of the blind man before the Pharisees that "God heareth not sinners" was evidently a quotation from the Pharisees' creed and not a gospel precept. As all have sinned and come short of the glory of God, no one would be heard if God would not hear sinners.

Here are a few of the testimonies which have a bearing on this important subject. One hardened sinner was so convicted of his completely lost condition that he spent the night in agony, calling on God for forgiveness. He was determined to fight the battle alone, but his strength failed and he was certain that he was condemned irrevocably to eternal punishment. His prayer availed him nothing. When, at last, he opened his heart to a faithful friend, that friend's prayer was heard instantaneously, and the seeker knew by an instinct axiomatic that he was received by the Lord.

There is a general belief that God does hear the pure person more readily than he does the vile reprobate. That belief is founded in the moral laws universally recognized in human relations. There may also be a semi-scientific reason. The soul which is in tune with the Infinite can more effectively detect and understand the "sound waves" from the spirit world than the soul which is out of tune with God. In the mass of the correspondence about which this book is written there are strong testimonies to the necessity and attainableness of a practical harmony with the Spirit of God. One man who has been long a teacher of psychology wrote that he had made a deliberate test of the matter, and a condensed report of his experience is here given.

He sought "to place his soul in communion with God." He desired that state of spiritual harmony with the divine character which would make him sensitive to every spiritually divine impression. Hence, he prepared himself in this way: he locked himself in his room and gave himself up to the serious business of getting into communication with God. He began to count his sins of commission and earnestly asking forgiveness; he promised the Lord that he would guard himself against them evermore. He then tried to comprehend the awful list of sins of omission which for a while made him hopeless of God's favor. But in deep and prayerful meditation, thin king long on the great mercy of God, he felt his soul slowly emerge from the slough of despond. Suddenly a strange confidence took possession of his soul and a feeling of glad triumph overcame all doubt of his forgiveness. The assurance that he was getting into harmony with the Spirit of God became complete. He threw himself across his bed and "let go of himself," making an absolute surrender to the spiritual impressions.

Into such a state the prophets must have entered to feel the spiritual impulses and see the visions which they recorded. It as an exaltation of the whole being- a temporarily superhuman experience which may be the state of the soul when released from the body. The joy of that hour of oneness with God cannot be described to one who has not known it. It is higher, purer, more real than other feelings. It is so unlike any other experience on earth.

"The soul is lost in God." The worshiper is outside and above himself. Life gleams as a cloud glows in some heavenly morning. Disease, pain, human limitations, care, or anxiety is nonexistent. A pure peace which passeth all understanding permeates the whole being. But why should he try to convey an idea of that growing answer to his prayer? He knows he is with his Lord. But the less he tries to tell his experience the more confidence his unbelieving friends will have in his sanity.

That such harmony with the divine is subject to certain laws is seen in the fact that such elevation of soul is gained only by a full compliance with certain conditions. Some of these conditions are found by experience to be those which are laid down in the Scriptures. The seeker must force out of his heart all malice, jealousy, hate, selfishness, covetousness, unbelief, and give himself up to the opposite feelings. We must go over wholly to pure intentions, holy aspirations, truth-living, kindness, forgiveness, love for all, inflexible adherence to the right, and all in all harmonizing with the divine disposition. Pure holiness must be sought, without which no man can please God. All those who give themselves over to such a state of surrender to God have the full assurance of faith which is promised to those who love God with all their hearts and with all their minds.

Such servants of God can offer prayer which avail much more than the frightened call of the worldly minded, egotistic, and selfish enemy of good people and good principles. God loves all men with an everlasting affection. But the kind of intensity of his affection for the saint and the transgressor is quite different. God never fails to hear the cry of any contrite heart, but the Good Samaritan is especially beloved.

Chapter XIV - Conflicting Prayers

THIS chapter leads into the wilderness. Just beyond it is the insane asylum. The most bewildering, confusing, and dangerous region is the morass of conflicting prayers. No human theory concerning them is even helpful. The labyrinth is absolutely trackless to the human mind when once the worshiper becomes entangled therein. So we will not attempt to explain any of the even unthinkable intricacies of its strange region. Nowhere in the Bible does the Lord answer the questions which millions have asked about it. Two persons, equally sincere, pray for success in a matter where the victory of one must be the defeat of the other. Nations at war pray hard and long for victory, and not even God can answer both. Something must be taken from one to give to another, while the one in possession is praying that he may keep it. One's loss is another's gain. The employer prays for a profit on his business, and the laborer prays for higher wages. The white man and the colored man prays for his own tribe.

Many an honest investigator has entered this region of doubt and mystery and managed to back out while still in his right mind. But he has returned the worse for the experience. All sorts of foolish speculations have been given creedal expression until men have declared, with strange assurance, that man cannot trust his reason or his conscience in any matter. They have tried to prove that the laws of nature are inflexible and that prayer cannot have any influence whatever in current events. Gifted men and women of culture and high purpose have convinced themselves that there is no evil, that men never sin, that the Bible theories concerning prayer are fanciful and too miraculous to be possible. The religious maniacs are those men who have broken down their brains by laborious study over these insoluble problems.

Therefore, while no one should discourage reasonable research anywhere, and while it is not sacrilegious or foolish to think on these things, it does seem best to admit that to the most faithful person there are unsearchable things of God which he cannot sanely hope to understand in this life. "My thoughts are not your thoughts, neither are your ways my ways, saith the Lord, For as the heavens are higher than the earth, so are my ways higher than your ways, and my thoughts higher than your thoughts."

We cannot expect to achieve a knowledge as great and extensive as that of the Creator, and must be content with our reasonable limitations. "What I do ye know not now, but ye shall know hereafter." Satisfied, then, with the promise of that future full revelation we should study all that Providence places before us for investigation and never let go of what we are sure we do know. We will distinguish, as clearly as possible, between our imagination and our knowledge, and with a level head and our feet on solid ground we will live by a faith that is reasonable and never become blindly reckless.

The lightning struck a tree near a neighbor's residence last week. He knows that to be a hard fact. He does not know much about the electric currents in the atmosphere, neither does the most experienced scientist; but the neighbor knows that the lightning did splinter that tree. From that fact he entertains a faith in a possible return of that event and by faith he puts up a lightning rod on his barn. The observer notices that sin brings its own punishment in many cases, and he has faith that such will be the universal experience of the future. So he keeps his soul insured by safe and sane investment in righteousness.

Every sane man knows that we must at all times walk largely by faith. Faith is a constituent part of the natural human constitution. The degree of faith determines the character of the individual. Faith, like water, seeks its level. But the greater its safe elevation, the greater its power. Faith must grow reasonably, like a grain of mustard seed. It also develops mysteriously by natural increase until the fowls of the air nest in its branches and its growing root will cleave off the side of the mountain. The patriot, earnestly seeking victory, lets no possible agency pass unused to overcome the enemy. When he has prepared fully and laboriously for the battle he will then pray for the help which God may give him. Even should he strongly doubt that the Great Power moving on events beyond his knowledge can or will hear him, yet he will not fail to pray.

Any man who calls on God will not ask him to aid an unholy cause. A murderer seeking an opportunity to kill will not call on God for aid. The thief ever fears some providential interference with his plans. The religious person ever hopes for God's aid, and asks for it because his aim is a godly one.

Herein is found the safe position for the believer to take. We can pray for the heathen, although they do pray against their own good. We can pray for victory in some holy war, because the enemy are praying really against their own good. Because their cause is unrighteous, their victory would be a great loss to them. Hence, even the great prayers which sublimely petition for the nations, and which include the whole world in their range of vision, are consistent only when man realizes his weakness and his ignorance, and adds to every prayer the reservation, "nevertheless, not my will but thine be done."

He is the wisest servant of God who can pray from the camp that he may conquer if his cause be really just. The preacher who enters his pulpit with an almost agonizing prayer that God would aid him in his presentation must ever ask that God will turn aside any arrow which would do harm to the cause. In his ignorance or weakness he may mistake the Divine message, or may not present the whole truth, and he must ever ask that, whether he gain or lose in the esteem of his congregation, the truth shall always prevail. Christian nations are often wrong in their diplomacy or in their wars, as they discover after a while. The Lord, therefore, gave them that for which they would have asked had their hearts been right with God and their intention been Godlike toward men.

Sometime we shall understand. But now the seeming inconsistency of asking the Lord to aid his own cause is ever a stumbling block to the doubtful ones. If the Lord has all power and has a sincere desire to make the world good, why does he not do it by one sweep of his hand or by one magic word? What is the reason for his commandment to pray to him and to ask him to do that which he wishes to do and can do himself? All these questions lead into the wilderness. We do not know. We cannot suggest any hypothesis which would make the sovereignty of God and the free will of man reconcilable. Man's mind is so constructed that it is impossible to believe that the Creator controls all things and arranges the details of even our thoughts and yet leaves man free to choose to defeat the Lord by his own thoughts and actions. It is impossible fully to believe that man can voluntarily do evil without in some way interfering with the designs and power of God. If God undertakes to save the world, and "would not that any should perish," but that all should come unto him and live, and yet sinful man can defeat or hinder the accomplishment of this purpose, then the thinker must conclude that God is not supreme.

Yet when we keep our minds within their reasonable limits and fall back on our common sense, we must believe that God is all-powerful and also that man is free to be sinful. The facts are actual facts, although we cannot reconcile them. There is but little we frail mortals can understand about such matters.

Let us, therefore, carefully hold to the facts which we can comprehend, and never assume that things which are, surely are not, or that things which are not, most surely are. There was a boulder in the highway yesterday. We don't know how it came to be there. We know it should not be there. But there it is, and he would be idiotic who tried to go on as if the stone were not there. Behold! There is set before every man good and evil. "Choose good that thou and thy seed may live." We know that in a thousand matters we can choose the good or choose the evil. We see also that liberty is limited by great laws and there are a myriad of things a man cannot possibly do and about which he has no choice. When a man reaches those limitations his responsibility for choosing ceases.

With these simple facts the teaching of the Bible is fully in accord. The necessity for sustenance and protection beyond our ability to supply is ever a great apparent fact. The recognition of that fact leads the thoughtful man to prayer. Let us, therefore, have a care not to venture too far into the wilderness of the seeming theological inconsistencies. That God does answer men and women, thousands can testify. They have tried it fully. They cannot explain why God thus works out his complicated schedules, but they know that he does work in that way. It is established fact.

Our great forefathers also prayed. That is enough.

Chapter XV - Subconscious Religion

IN Leipzig, Germany, in 1866 there stood an old three-story mansion, used as a manufactory of mechanical toys. An American student attending the university was invited to visit the showrooms in the upper story and became intently interested in the surprising exhibition of inventive genius. As the visitor descended to the second and first floors he visited the rooms where machinery of many kinds was turning out various parts of the toys. But when he ventured to descend to the cellar to look at the power plant he found "No admission" on every door. But he was more disappointed when he was told that the "designing room," where the toys were invented and the drawings made, was in the sub-cellar. In order to preserve their patents and their secret processes, even the workmen on the upper floors were forbidden ever to look into the sub-cellar.

That illustrative fact came forcibly to mind when meditating long over a letter written by a praying student and author who said that he felt sure that the only direct passage between the human soul and the world spirits is through the subconscious mind. From that sub-cellar of the soul come ideas, impulses, and suggestions which most largely influence our actions. But we are forbidden to enter that department to examine the plans or listen to the wireless dispatches from the spirit world so continuously received there. "No admission" is posted on every door to the sub-cellar designing room of the human soul. We get the blueprints of new plans, or read suggestions for new or improved work sent up to our brains. But who makes them we do not know. In the impenetrable regions of our mental and spiritual nature are formulated many ideas and moral laws which we must blindly obey.

A man is what he thinks, and the larger portion of his thinking is originated or molded in his subconscious self. It is amazing to the careful student of our mental constitution to find out how meager is the part of our thinking which originates in the suggestions of our five senses. From the Grecian and German philosophers some psychologists derived the hypothesis that the subconscious self is only the aggregation of all the faint or half-formed ideas which are not strong enough to force themselves up into full recognition by the brain. Consciousness includes only those thoughts which the brain accepts and uses in positive action. That theory seems to be, in a measure, true. There are faint suggestions and half-formed motives of which we catch glimpses and which never seem to be fully developed. Also the natural instincts of our animal nature still continue and persist in our higher station in the creative order. It can be noted by anyone that perhaps not one in a thousand of our muscular contractions or of our decided actions is consciously dictated by our will. The human race is seemingly, in a large measure, a collection of automatons. We are generally moved about by powers and mechanisms beyond our comprehension and are unconsciously working out designs in the making of which we live no consciously important part.

It is difficult to write clearly on such a subtle theme or explain what is known concerning autosuggestion or explain the laws which, in a measure, control the unconscious part of human life without using technical terms or scientific formulas beyond the understanding of the everyday reader. But, plainly stated, a human being uses but a small inclosure in which he can move on his own conscious volition. We are fearfully and wonderfully made. "What I would not that I do and what I would that I do not" is the common experience of all mankind. A man's thoughts, happiness, and usefulness are the products of his moral character. His "subconscious self" is his real character. What one does consciously may not represent his real character, but that which he does without meditation or conscious limitation represents the true disposition or tendency of his real nature. The redeemed soul is one whose permanent disposition, called his "subconscious " or " subliminal self ," is controlled by the magnetic influence of the spirit of truth and goodness.

The few matters on which the brain acts directly are the deeds of the conscious mind. They are controlled by the will and reasoning powers of the independent portion of man's being. They may or may not accord with the heart's general impulses or they may be the direct product of the heart's purposes. The will and the subconscious self interact, each influencing the other. This thought presents a logical contradiction which has puzzled many great minds.

But our appeal here is to the everyday experience of sincere, truthful people concerning their communication with God through the subconscious mind. One writer states that she has often received trustworthy messages from the spirit world in dreams and in unusual impressions during waking hours. This statement often arouses the general prejudice which some of the extreme spiritualists or deceivers have brought upon the theory of mental communication with the departed; but it should be examined on its own merits without bias. The testimony of the millions who believe or hope that they have had messages from their beloved who have gone on before counts for much and is not a testimony confined to professional mediums. The rejection of the theory that it is possible for angel beings to communicate with mortals, and that they are sent of God to do so, involves the rejection of the whole Bible as a divinely truthful Book. If there is no open path through the subconscious self to the spirit world, then the recorded visits of the Holy Spirit to the hearts of men are only idle tales. The disbelief in the soul's ability to hear heavenly voices or receive spiritual suggestions from other spirits would destroy all trust in supernatural religions. God does speak to man in the events and laws of the material life, and he also speaks to us in the "quiet, small voice" as he did to Elijah at Sinai. There appears to be no alternative but to believe in that declaration, for to reject it is to reject the whole body of religious teaching. We will not entertain such a suicidal proposition.

The indestructible spirit body is the same being and possesses the same characteristics in the material body that it possesses when separated from this limiting framework of the earthly body. It is indestructible, but it can be modified in disposition while in this body. That statement, for the sake of brevity, is mentioned dogmatically, but it will be illustrated by the following testimonials.

One writer who evidently has been reared to believe sincerely in "emotional religion," who shouts and groans and wrings his hands at any devotional meeting, but whose probity and strong good sense are the admiration of his friends, states that he knows "that his Redeemer liveth, by the direct assurance of the Spirit." He claims that when a man tells him a lie he feels the presence of evil. He testifies that in his most exalted moments following a season of fervent prayer he knows what it is to realize the fact that he lives and moves and has his being in God.

There are thousands of men and women whose wild behavior in religious meetings is only the natural evidence of it disordered mind. The Negro camp meeting and the whirling of the Egyptian dervishes seem to be much alike in their manner of working up a religious excitement. The unbalanced mental condition of some truly honest worshipers causes distrust of others whose good sense in other matters is never questioned.

Other writers tell of their experience of some overpowering emotion which came so logically in answer to their prayer that they cannot doubt that such was truly the fact. A man prayed that he might be protected through the night. He awakened from sleep, moved by an "inward impulse" irresistible, and went to the barn to find, as he opened the stable door, a little blaze creeping toward the haymow. It was easily extinguished then, but ten minutes later would have been entirely beyond control. The fire was caused by a lighted cigar dropped carelessly on the stable floor near the horses.

Another writes that he is naturally emotional and dares not trust himself on any pinnacle, as he always feels when on any high place a strange desire to leap off in suicide. He states that the sensitiveness of his emotional nature becomes most acute in religious gatherings, and that he has never found himself mistaken when he has followed the leadings of that spirit. His wife writes that he had, for years, planted the crops which "he felt like planting" after attending a religious meeting. She adds that while, at first, she had regarded his " moods " as accidental emotions, she had learned that his crops planted in those moods were always profitable investments.

Another who had been trained in the Friends' meeting to wait for the Spirit to move him went so far as to wait for the same impulse in all his undertakings. He tried to lay his business ventures before the Lord in silent prayer and then go in the direction the Spirit indicated. He related how, when once he was lost in a thick forest on a cloudy day, he prayed until his "sense of direction" became so clear that he started with closed eyes to take the direction toward which his inward impression impelled him. Another acted always on the impulse of the moment in speaking to a friend or to a stranger upon religious matters. Another wrote that she had observed for many years that the praying housekeepers were guided in their work by the most trustworthy intuitions. Few is the number of women who guide their domestic affairs by the rules of cold science, and the larger part of a mother's movements in the care of her children are the unconscious results of special intuition. She claims that in the intuitional nature of the human soul there is such nearness to the divine nature that the especially sensitive soul "feels impulses from across the border."

Here, again, after a day's study of the many accounts concerning the impulses awakened by prayer, we lay down the correspondence with a sigh of regret that nothing absolutely conclusive for or against prayer is to be found. We must still believe or disbelieve according to the measure of faith. In the courts of law attorneys often establish their cases by the use of what is termed " cumulative evidence," where they secure the testimony of many witnesses to the same fact. If that custom be applied to the establishment of the fact that emotions and impulses are sent in answer to prayer the number in its favor would be overwhelming. Down in the sub-cellar of the mind there may be a tunnel leading through to the palace of God. Millions believe that is a fact. No one can prove it is not so. Therefore, with the reasonable student, the testimony of the many will still be considered trustworthy. The soul of God speaketh often to the soul of man. A great writer on secular subjects confirmed the general impression when he forcibly wrote, "You can get almost anything you want, if you only want it hard enough, and long enough, and with faith enough."

Chapter XVI - Praying for Visions of Heaven

A STURDY, young farmer's boy who had inherited a. strong body, a clear mind, and a good family name sat under a maple tree in the hayfield at the hot noontide. He was eating a cold lunch and at the same time reading an article in the weekly paper. The editor had written an editorial on the romantic history of the poor country boys who had risen to world-wide fame and to enormous riches. When he had reread the article he tossed the paper aside, lay back on the odorous new-mown grass, looked up at the deep-blue sky, and watched the passing of a pure-white cloud. A vision of what the world might be to him came in a dreamy way. Other boys as poor as he had graduated from college, had made great scientific discoveries, had married rich and beautiful women, had traveled in far countries, had feasted with kings, had held high office, and had written great books.

Why could not he follow their example? It seemed impossible, and with a deep sigh he arose and seized his scythe.

But the vision could not be obscured. As his strong muscles drove the sharp blade through the thick grass he kept muttering to himself, debating pro and con the possibility of an ignorant farmer, living far away from city civilization, and too far from a railroad to hear the whistle, to become powerful in national affairs. How did they start? What did they do first? When his return swath brought him again near the shade of the tree where he had eaten his lunch he caught up the weekly paper and read again the editorial. Then he left his scythe in the grass and went into the shade, leaned against the gnarled trunk of the old tree, and, wholly engrossed in earnest thought, forgot his work. He reviewed his own simple life and examined his own plans and ambitions. He had expected to marry some one of the strong, sensible, country girls and bring her home to live with the old folks, as his father had done. He had a dim idea that he would inherit the old, stony farm some day. He had a latent ambition to raise more corn than his father had raised and to clear a large piece of woodland which for centuries had hidden the mountain side. He would build an addition to the stable and put in a new pair of bars near the brook where the cattle went to drink in winter. He had also a half-formed purpose to join the local church, and perhaps some day he would be an elder.

At last he aroused himself and, with a half-angry impulse, he began to strike the grass with his scythe as if the grass were some sneaking enemy. He could not arouse again the sweet content of the forenoon. He had caught a glimpse of that far-away land, and while he did not hope ever to enter it, yet the thought disturbed him.

The next Sunday the echo of the old church bell, along the narrow, but beautiful, Berkshire valleys, called him to church. The cows were milked and fed, the old horse curried, and the chores hastily finished when he ran down the road to overtake the old folks. But the grand forest, the sheening, cascading brook, and the brown fields were not the same to him that they were the day before. The cows and horses in the pastures near the road had lost their fascination and value. The hills seemed lower and the grain fields more narrow, the cottages seemed shrunken, and the old church was but an awkwardly built bungalow. All had changed. His clothing was coarser woven and the most attractive girls in their Sunday attire were rude specimens of country verdancy.

As if by a preconceived purpose to accelerate his sweeping mental changes the preacher that morning took his text from the Proverbs of Solomon, wherein he stated that wisdom is more valuable than gold or rubies. The speaker illustrated his sermon by showing the value of an education. He mentioned the happiness of the men and women who knew the structure of vegetation, of animals, and the laws which control their life. He mentioned cases of self-made men who had read good books and whose minds could walk with God through his wonderful natural creations. He spoke of the uselessness or curse of possessions which the owner cannot enjoy for lack of knowledge. He said that the discipline of obtaining wisdom was in itself of great value and that God promised riches and honor to the man who would earn them. He also said that the Lord started many of us into life with nothing for the loving purpose of developing our capacity and inclination to know and enjoy more. The happiest boy is the one who makes his own toys. The application of the sermon brought forth the exhortation to read instructive books, to examine more closely the works of nature and the laws which control our being. "Learn something every day," said the preacher.

The young farmer was an only son, but his parents had wisely kept him from selfishness and egotism. He had been taught to work and to be grateful for the necessities of life. He had a loyal disposition and loved his parents with a half-worshipful devotion. He had been contented, industrious, careful, and honest. His only pride seemed to be in the distance he could see and in the large burden he could shoulder or carry. He had left school because his father needed him on the farm and he had abandoned the expectation of further education. But on that Sunday he held a long conference with his mother and father concerning his ambition to be something more than a country farmer. He read to them the editorial which had so moved him, and tearfully said: "I want to be great like them! I must improve my mind. I must increase my skill. I must have more influence and do more good. I must get more wisdom and more understanding. This farm is too small a place for me. I will stay at home if I can, or as long as I can, but I must begin to study tomorrow, and never thereafter lose a day. God helping me, I will be something worthwhile."

His parents, with sad hearts, saw the reasonableness of his ambition and gave their consent to his proposed education. He began to read selected books at home, but he soon saw the great advantage of academic instruction in some well-equipped institution. He attended a high school in a near-by village and an academy in another part of the country. He was the leader of his classes and a close student of languages and natural science. He had obtained a glimpse of the world of knowledge and was fascinated with the idea of a university education. Beyond the university, he occasionally saw himself a multimillionaire with a palace and a brilliant retinue of servants. He had chosen for his life mate a brilliant young woman who was a teacher in a kindergarten school connected with the academy. They were to be married when he should graduate from the university. All seemed hopeful and promised a most noble and notable career.

But while he was spending his vacation at the old home in the Hampshire Highlands of the Berkshire Hills, helping his old father in gathering the usual crops, he received an invitation from a rich uncle living near San Francisco, inviting him to visit his estate. The uncle had not often corresponded with the young man's parents and they had taken no interest in his history. They had heard that he was a wealthy manufacturer and a railroad director. So the brother, and the sister who was the student's mother, had lost all acquaintance with each other in the fifty years of their separation. The young man gladly accepted his uncle's invitation to visit him, and the uncle sent on a railroad pass to bring him to California and return.

The estate of the uncle was on the shore of the Pacific, occupying a gentle slope with wide lawns, evergreen trees fancifully trimmed, and gushing fountains. Hedges of lilies, acres of poppies, roses of every perennial variety, and shade trees in long rows, decorated the great plateau. Orchards of luscious and rare fruits stretched away in great lanes from the back gardens. The house was a mansion built for show, with a front largely Grecian in design, and a rear porch and veranda of the Old Colony style. Carpets, paintings, mirrors, and a hundred curious and costly decorations made an exhibition of lavish wealth. Fine horses and extravagantly furnished carriages in great variety filled the stables. Servants' quarters were really fine cottages and the gatekeeper's lodge cost an extravagant sum.

To this New England nephew who had spent his youth in the simplicity and poverty of a back-country farm, all this display of wealth was bewildering. The great library of costly volumes, few of which had ever been opened, seemed to him a great opportunity for his uncle to learn almost everything. The food was so various and so delicious. The wines which he had never tasted were sweetly stimulating and had been made on the estate. His uncle entertained him royally and introduced him to a number of handsome young ladies of fascinating manners, who volunteered to teach him to dance. Every kind of musical invention seemed to be stored in the mansion, and quartets from the university near by came in often to entertain and to be entertained at the uncle's evening socials. The uncle was a widower and childless, and seemed to be most pathetically lonely. He was pleased with his nephew and was proud of his apparently sterling character and manly appearance.

The evening before the nephew's departure on his return journey his uncle talked with him until late in the night and told him frankly that he was going to make the young man his sole heir. But he made his nephew promise repeatedly not to tell any person, not even his parents, what the uncle had decided to do. The return of that young man, when viewed in the light of subsequent events, must have been a startling experience to his dear, patient, plodding old parents. His manners, his thoughts, his estimation of values had undergone a violent change. The old farmhouse seemed to him to be smaller than ever, the furniture was rude and cheap, the food was coarse and unpalatable, the horse was shamefully old, his father's overalls were disgracefully stained, and his mother's old apron was fit only for rags! The home was lonesome and uncomfortable. He sat by the fire on the cool evenings, silently picturing in his wild imagination what he would do with his millions, and sometimes he admitted, for an instant, the hope that his uncle would die very soon. He abandoned the idea of going on with his college education. He reasoned that money can buy anything and assured himself that he could hire men to think for him if he should need them. Letters from his fiancée became a bore. She was too plain and too unsophisticated to adorn his future mansion. He could not think of marrying a woman of whom he would be ashamed in that fashionable group to which he would be attached. He finally broke the engagement, telling her that he had discovered that he did not love her enough sincerely to marry her. The lady became ill and was suddenly killed in an accident in the sanitarium. The young man would not work. He refused to help his father on the old place and bluntly refused to help his mother when she was about her household tasks alone. All was changed. He was no longer their son. The father felt the impression of mystery about the son's strange behavior and suggested to his wife that the boy showed symptoms of insanity.

Not many months passed before the son left his home to take an easy position as a clerk in Boston, but he soon left that and went to sea in a steamer, where he acted as assistant to the steward. At Bordeaux, France, he made the acquaintance of two American young men whose wealthy parents supplied them with funds to travel, but evidently did so to keep the rascals away from home. Then his downward course became a reckless race.

A few years later the uncle heard or read that his nephew was sentenced to three months in the workhouse for drunkenness, and he changed his will, leaving all his estate to benevolent institutions. From that time the unrepentant prodigal disappeared from the knowledge or care of his old neighbors. Both his parents went down to the grave in bitter sorrow before his reform. The death of the mother was only a few weeks later than the death of the father.

God pity them both, God pity us all,
Who vainly the dreams of youth recall.
Of all sad words of tongue or pen
The saddest are these, "It might have been."
Ah, well for us all some sweet hope lies
Deeply hidden from human eyes,
And in the hereafter the angels may
Roll the stone from the grave away.

The friend who reads this account of that young man's broken life may ask what this biographical sketch has to do with the subject of "unanswered prayer." It has much to do with it. Such experiences, which must have been seen in millions of cases, show a reasonable explanation why so many prayers for a view of heaven are denied. At almost every funeral the loved ones ask if the departed is still living and why God does not permit them to come back and tell us about their spirit life. "What are they doing in heaven?" is a question on the lips of millions. But in the letters herein mentioned the records of unanswered prayers include many who prayed for visions of heaven or who wished to see the angels. One brother prayed continually, "Oh, for one view of the holy city!" and another seemed never to leave out of his daily prayer, "Lord, open my eyes to see the faces of the dear ones hovering about me!" But our eyes are still holden. Our pleading hearts are unsatisfied. We are not permitted to see our future home nor catch more than a glimpse of the angels' wings. When, however, we seek an explanation of this divine arrangement, this separation of this life from the other, the faithful believer in God's wisdom and love can easily set up a reasonable theory concerning it. He will see that God has placed us on this earth to grow in knowledge, to get necessary spiritual discipline for his heavenly service. To obtain that training we must keep our attention on the duties of our daily tasks and do them well. We cannot reap rye with heaven in actual view.

When that California uncle showed his nephew all that luxury, beauty, and wealth, and told him that he would some day own it all, it was a foolish act - almost criminal. The young man's mental and moral development was stopped then and there. The young man lost far more than the estate could be worth. Suddenly acquired riches are ever harmful. Dissatisfaction with this life is a fatal sin. God commands us to be content and toil. He, therefore, does not himself do so destructive and discouraging an act as to show us heaven's glories and fill us with a suicidal anxiety to get out of this world at once and speedily to enter the other where there is no more pain or sorrow or dying. A prayer for a view of heaven seems, therefore, to be an unreasonable request. This conclusion satisfies many who have been denied communication with the departed dear ones, and they take up their toil, content to labor and to wait. God does not interfere with the healthful exercise of our free will by holding bribes before our eyes or by forcing our discipline by awful fears.

Chapter XVII - Great Prayers

MEN talk and write of "great prayers" as though such petitions could be weighed or measured. They appear to think that sacred feelings can find a standard of comparison. But even the rightfully esteemed Lord's Prayer presents no universal standard by which to measure our varying appeals. One old saint writes that he often gets out of patience when the Lord's Prayer is intoned or recited, as none of its paragraphs fitly or adequately expresses his "soul's sincere desire."

Prayer is necessarily as varying in its moods and objects as a kaleidoscope. We must pray, but person, time, place, hearers, sharers, emotions, ideas, desires, and needs all enter into the conditions of earnest prayer. To call on God in your own way, with your own motives and your own emotions and your own language, or without words, will be a clear fulfillment of the command to pray. The Lord understands every language and knows all that the heart would express if it could find an adequate form of speech.

The books, except the Bible, most frequently quoted in these letters include volumes by St. Augustine, Luther, Wesley, Whitfield, Spurgeon, Moody, Fosdick, Nicoll, Campbell, Whittle, and Finney. In the quotations the idea is ever present that there are great prayers. But it is misleading to attempt to place a valuation on any of them, for there are an almost innumerable number of cases where prayers brought direct results although there was no attempt to use any special form of words.

This principle or truth is probably accepted by all thinking worshipers, including most extreme ritualists. As, however, true prayer requires a devotional state of mind there can be no denial of the statement that the forms, ceremonials, scenic effects, and processions of the different creeds and races have a most potent effect on the devotional natures of their supporters. Whatever awakens a spirit of devotion is more or less useful; but when a strong desire for communion with God has been aroused by music, exhortation, processions, or scenery, the most effective method appears to be to then leave each soul alone with God in silent prayer. Love only can understand love. To be "alone with the loved one" is ever a holy and soul-brightening experience. But to be "alone with God" is, by far, the most holy of all emotions. The testimony of nearly all those at the Baptist Temple who report an answer to prayer, mention the fact that their prayers seemed to be the most productive of results when offered in the silent moments at the close of some inspiring service.

It is clearly impossible for one finite mind to shape a petition which will include and express all the desires of the multitude. Neither can an uninspired writer in one age fully appreciate and comprehend the conditions and needs of another age. Hence, while the petitions of friends, priests, or pastors have a strong influence with the Creator, the one vital necessity in making acceptable appeals to God is that each petitioner should ask for himself. No character can be changed from the outside. No wicked heart can be made pure without its own consent, and the Lord seems to have limited himself so that he never crosses the threshold of the soul unless he is sincerely invited by that individual householder. God does not convert any soul by force. Therefore, all who would be blessed by him must voluntarily and individually go to him. There can be no substitute in that case.

Chapter XVIII - Use of the Bible in Prayer

IT will be useful to any seeker after God to examine the agencies which have helped those whose prayers have been conspicuously answered. Among the many helps which, seemingly, have had especial potency in developing or awakening a devout spirit there is none so general in use as the Bible. The petitions which have been preserved from the ancient Fathers often quote the Scriptures; and when they do not quote directly, the language used shows a close familiarity with the Sacred Word.

The following is a wonderful prayer by Thomas B. Kempis:

O, Most merciful Lord, grant me thy grace, that it may be with me, and labor within me, and persevere with me, even to the end. Grant that I may always desire and will that which is to thee most acceptable, and most dear. Let thy will be mine, and my will ever follow thine and agree perfectly with it. Grant to me, above all things that can be desired, to rest in thee, and thee to have my heart at peace. Thou art the true peace of the heart, thou its only rest; out of thee all things are hard and restless. In this very peace, that is, in thee the one Chiefest Eternal Good, I will sleep and rest.
Amen.

It can be seen clearly that those whose petitions were the most surely answered were familiar with the Bible. It is also interesting to notice the quotations which were used as mottoes or the favorite extracts from the Bible by the most saintly of the heroes, martyrs, and victors. Out of many hundreds of Scripture quotations the following are selected with the hope that some one of them may be of especial helpfulness to someone who desires to pray successfully:

Hear me when I call, O God of my righteousness; thou hast enlarged me when I was in distress; have mercy upon me, and hear my prayer (Psalm iv :1).

My voice shalt thou hear in the morning, O Lord; in the morning will I direct my prayer unto thee, and will look up (Psalm v:3).

The Lord hath heard my supplication; the Lord will receive my prayer (Psalm vi 9).

Give ear to my prayer, O God; and hide not thyself from my supplication (Psalm iv:l).

Let my prayer be set forth before thee as incense; and the lifting up of my hands as the evening sacrifice (Psalm cxli:2).

Yet have thou respect unto the prayer of thy servant, and to his supplication, O Lord my God, to hearken unto the cry and to the prayer, which thy servant prayeth before thee today (I Kings viii:28).

And whiles I was speaking, and praying, and confessing my sin and the sin of my people Israel, and presenting my supplication before the Lord my God for the holy mountain of my God; Yea, whiles I was speaking in prayer, even the man Gabriel, whom I had seen in the vision at the beginning, being caused to fly swiftly, touched me about the time of the evening oblation (Dan. ix:20-21).

And hearken thou to the supplication of thy servant, and of thy people Israel, when they shall pray toward this place: and hear thou in heaven thy dwelling place: and when thou hearest, forgive (I Kings viii:30).

Nevertheless, we made our prayer unto our God, and set a watch against them day and night, because of them (Neh. iv:9).

Thou shalt make thy prayer unto him, and he shall hear thee, and thou shalt pay thy vows (Job xxii 97).

He will regard the prayer of the destitute, and not despise their prayer (Psalm cii:17).

The sacrifice of the wicked is an abomination to the Lord; but the prayer of the upright is his delight (Prov. xv :8).

And I set my face unto the Lord God, to seek by prayer and supplications, with fasting, and sackcloth, and ashes . . . (Dan. ix:3).

Trust in the Lord, and do good; so shalt thou dwell in the land, and verily thou shalt be fed (Psalm xxxvii:3).

Commit thy way unto the Lord; trust also in him; and he shall bring it to pass (Psalm Xxxvii:5).

Rest in the Lord, and wait patiently for him . . . (Psalm xxxvii:7).

The Lord is my shepherd; I shall not want (Psalm xxii:1).

Yea, though I walk through the valley of the shadow of death, I will fear no evil; for thou art with me; thy rod and thy staff they comfort me (Psalm xxiii:4).

Chapter XIX - Conclusions

AS one lays aside the last letter of this collection and leans back in his chair for meditation on all these heart revelations he asks, most anxiously, What is the conclusion of the whole matter?

Thanks be unto God who giveth us the victory, our faith remains unmoved. A general view of the field of prayer shows that the great fundamental facts remain undisturbed. God is. God answers prayer. The Bible is the inspired work of the Spirit of God. Entering upon this investigation with a firm determination to hold an unbiased mind and trying to examine the evidence as an impartial judge, there were moments of doubt as to the wisdom of setting one's mind so free. It seemed sometimes as if it was wrong, even for a day, to stand outside of the circle of earnest believers and be a neutral critic of sacred things. But the risk was taken. A tremor came with the suggestion that the lovely structure of our lifelong faith might be shattered, and only dust be left of the religious building which we had so fondly believed was a building that had indestructible foundations, "Eternal in the heavens."

But not one pillar has moved, not a rent or seam in any of the old walls has appeared. The fear that faith might be lost has increased our estimate of its everlasting value. The faith of our fathers stands secure. The mistakes, errors, and superstitions of the extremists and deceivers have not made more than a ripple in the current of religious faith. The tide comes back. The love for the Holy Bible revives. The prodigal will come to himself and come back. The spirit of religion is a necessity to human progress and human happiness. The world needs it. It may come slowly, but, nevertheless, it will come surely. The spirit will awaken. The winter cannot last forever. Prayer is as necessary to the spirit of man as breath is to his body. The soul's sincere desire will ever seek expression. The seeker after God will surely find him when he shall truly seek him with all his heart.

Hundreds testified to the facts that their prayers were answered where only a score or less asserted that they did not know whether their requests were heard or not. The millions who never tried to pray cannot be accepted as witnesses on either side. But the great majority of those who have tried the matter testify to its effectiveness. The doubters, who quibble and stumble over the parables and miracles, find that whether the believer accepted them as literal history or as spiritual illustrations, they all teach the truth; and to believe in them can do no harm. The consensus of religious opinion among the common people is decidedly in favor of trusting more and, consequently, doubting less.

Right is Right, since God is God,
And right the day will win;
To doubt would be disloyalty,
To falter would be sin.

Ye saints, with your faith of steel, pray on. Ye faltering sinners, smite your breast and pray on. Ye doubtful critics, pray on. Ye sorrow-stricken ones, pray on. In due time every petitioner shall reap if he or she faints not.

BN Publishing

Improving People's Life

www.bnpublishing.com

www.ingramcontent.com/pod-product-compliance
Lightning Source LLC
Chambersburg PA
CBHW032140040426
42449CB00005B/335